EULOGIES TO DIE FOR

A BOOK FOR THOSE MOMENTS WHEN WORDS FAIL US

Patricia Dignan

authorHOUSE®

AuthorHouse™
1663 Liberty Drive, Suite 200
Bloomington, IN 47403
www.authorhouse.com
Phone: 1-800-839-8640

© 2008 Patricia Dignan. All rights reserved.

No part of this book may be reproduced, stored in a retrieval system, or transmitted by any means without the written permission of the author.

First published by AuthorHouse   8/14/2008

ISBN: 978-1-4343-8306-8 (sc)

Printed in the United States of America
Bloomington, Indiana

This book is printed on acid-free paper.

The author dedicates this book to those she loves and for whom she hopes she never has to give a eulogy.

If custom-made eulogies are desired within 36 hours of a loved one's death, contact the author, Dr. Patricia J. Dignan, by calling her at 734-485-3039 or through the Internet at pygmalion@provide.net or her webpage of eulogiestodiefor.com

INTRODUCTION

When I most wanted to find the right words to commemorate someone near and dear to me—at his or her death—was the very time that finding those special words became almost impossible. Between my grief and the inadequacy of the English alphabet, I found myself at a loss verbally with a fear that the very last thing I could do for someone I loved wasn't going to be done well—or, almost worse—would be done by someone else.

After a number of deaths of family and friends, I realized not knowing what to say at such a time was a common problem. I decided to write a book with categories for eulogies with interchangeable parts that anyone could use on short notice. Each can be used by itself or can be added to from other categories or from the religious and secular sections at the end of the book. Although each can stand on its own, I encourage readers to add their sentiments as well. Remember, whether using my words or yours, the most important attribute in eulogizing someone is the personal touch. Even humor may have a place in comments as you speak heartfelt grief over the body or the grave. Personalized words can sometimes bring as much comfort to the living as they bring tribute and recognition to the dead.

What follows are eulogies that can be generically applied or "cut and pasted" to suit circumstances and a particular person; I have used female and male pronouns alternately. You may want to combine words of your own with some of mine. Or you could draw from several headings in this book if they seem to fit. For example, if you had an aunt who was an antique dealer with a great sense of humor, you would look under Aunt, Antique Dealer, and Practical Joker. Similarly, if you don't find what you're looking for under Cleric, see Minister, Nun, Priest, or Rabbi. This book can assist you and those whose grief you are hoping to ameliorate even if only for a moment. In the final section are some very common and some not-so-common prayers, readings, sayings, and parts of hymns or well-known songs that may also be used effectively. As Phyllis Theroux wrote in her *Book of Eulogies*, "the eulogist is the first person to step forward, in a formal way, to hold a lantern above the loss". I believe the words used when holding that lantern matter far less than the love that comes shining through.

A well thought out eulogy is the last personal gift you can give your beloved and those who loved him or her. I sincerely hope I have assuaged some of that grief by helping you say, "**Fare Thee Well and God Speed**"

EULOGIES WRITTEN
OUT OF NECESSITY

The first eulogy I ever wrote was for our **Infant Son, Jimmy**, born severely handicapped, with no eyes, brain, nerves for hearing, or pituitary gland. Jimmy had to be tube fed. They said he'd never grow. He lived 6 months and tripled his birth weight—because we loved him.

Two years later, the eulogy I wrote for my **Mother** acknowledged that her life had been far from easy and her mothering—self-admittedly—far from perfect:

> *Our mother was an unusual woman. She was roughly gentle yet allowed her softness to show through only when dying. She wasn't the kind of mother to touch you with her hands instead she touched you with her intelligence, her resoluteness, and her ability to take care of only the things she could control and leave the rest to God.*
>
> *She had a hard life but glamorous dreams yet she never tried to live those dreams through us. She never pushed us to fulfill her dreams but prodded us to fulfill our own. I guess that's the best a mother can do. She said in March, "I wish you kids would think of me as a person instead of your mother because mothers are supposed to be perfect and I'm not...But if you kids would think of me just as a person, I know you'd like me because I have a lot of good qualities...." Mom was never one for flattery nor was she comfortable with*

praise. She thought we should know how much she cared for us by what she did not by what she said. And care for us she did!

Mom was probably the most honest person we'll ever know. Sometimes, painfully so, to the point of making us survivors in a critical world. Even when we were young and asked for her help in making decisions, she would never give us the answers—instead she gave us the ability and confidence to make the decision on our own. She taught us to be true to ourselves and that anything worth doing was worth doing well.

Mom was well read and well informed, often surprising a select few with her perspective and her perspicacity. She was more comfortable finding her place in a book than in a world among people because she could reach out to the words and they to her at her own pace and in her own time. She was a timid and modest person; never one to brag or boast. Not even about the accomplishments of those she loved best. And love she did! But in ways that mystified many of us who are used to listening to what people say instead of what they don't say. Last Tuesday, barely strong enough to whisper, she said, "None of us ever loves enough".

We probably didn't show Mom how much we loved her either until she was too weak to resist our touching or turn away from our endearments. In the last days, each of us held her hand and supported her part way on her final journey through this vale of tears and into the valley of death. Yet she led the way. Headstrong, nobly, and with unmatched courage, she exemplified the same determination to "get through it" as she had personified in life.

Death be not proud. She even made you wait until she was ready—at her own pace and in her own time. Don't think of hers as a life terminated, bur rather as a life complete. Between the brackets on her gravestone (May 16, 1922-September 2, 1988) lies a strong message of forgiveness and wisdom to know that each of us does the best we can with the cards we've been dealt.

Mom may you who were dealt so many cards feel that the Ultimate Trump was yours. And may you who were so full of energy and ambition, rest, finally, now, in peace. Now and forever. Amen.

Then came a eulogy for a very special lady, my **Mother-in-Law:**

Webster needed almost 2 paragraphs to define a Lady; I only need 2 words: Alice Dignan, otherwise known affectionately as Mum, Momma, or Allie. Alice Dignan was a lady—as she used to define one—"from the top of her head to the tip of her toes". She was gracious, charming and ageless. One of her favorite stories happened a few years ago when I was only in my thirties and I went to Senior Citizens with Dad and an old friend came up to us thinking I was Alice and said, "Why, Alice, you look younger every time I see you!" She got a chuckle out of that but she was a lady who could find fun in all of life's folibles.

She was ageless in other ways too. She kept up with the times while understanding the pressures and promises of youth. She would surprise you with her open mind and undaunted support for teenagers. She commiserated with them yet knew that sex, drugs, and rock and roll weighed heavily on their choices. If her grand kids needed an ally, she was the first to whom they'd run—knowing she'd take their side no matter the issue. In fact she had the talent of making you feel like she was on your side even when you were an in-law! I don't think she knew what in-law was supposed to mean—she thought it meant special gift and special family.

She was a lady of perspective never preaching faith, hope, and charity: She just lived them. Years before she became a convert, she'd take her son to daily Mass at 6:00 am so he could be an altar boy. But she had faith in the human race in general and a deeper compassion for others than anyone I've ever known. If you hurt, she hurt. She would cry over the ones she worried about yet be confident that the Lord would take care of them. She was a lady of faith and good works. And she was faithful to family and friends! She always thought of their feelings even at the times it would have been easier to think of her own. She treasured the people in her life and had the gift of making each feel special.. She could have all her loved ones in the same room at the same time yet make each one of them feel like they were her favorite. I've never known another human being who could do that and do it so meaningfully.

She was a lady with a real knack for knowing what to say and when to say it. And what a family person she was! Each of her kids had a lifetime of unconditional loving and always came first—until they were foolish enough to give her grand kids. She used to tell me, "Patricia, every crow thinks theirs it the blackest" but, boy, did she crow over her grand kids! She was a lady who will be sorely missed by all from "the top of her head to the tip of her toes". May you receive the rewards you have so justly earned, Mum, and may you know eternal peace. Amen

MY OWN EULOGY (DONE AHEAD OF TIME, HOPEFULLY, YEARS.....)

THERE ARE SO FEW CAN GROW OLD WITH GRACE AND I GUESS I'M NOT ONE OF THEM; OTHERWISE. WHY TAKE ME BEFORE I'M 100?

Rejoice *by Bridges (1844-1930)*

"Rejoice ye dead, where'er your spirits dwell,
Rejoice that yet on earth your fame is bright,
And that your names, remembered day and night,
Live on the lips of those who love you well.

Dear Lord,

I know I didn't live my life the way either of us intended but, hopefully, you'll welcome me into your kingdom anyway. ***St. Luke tells us:Her sins which are many are forgiven for she has loved much.***

An old English poem says, Doubt thou the stars are fire; Doubt that the sun doth move; Doubt truth to be a liar; But never doubt I love(d).

And loved I did—my family, some unforgettable men and women, my sisters and brothers, my friends and countless relatives, many whom I saw infrequently but held in my heart. The same heart that overflowed with smiles and tears and moments of self-doubt.

It may surprise those who knew me that I was pretty spiritual even though, regretfully, petty, and it may even surprise my family that You, Lord, and I had an ongoing conversation over the years. Even though you were pretty quiet, I was always aware of your presence. Unfortunately, Your reticence didn't inhibit me enough to keep me from some self-destructive behaviors (but even then I knew You were by my side, Lord). Whether taking a chance when the odds were against me or imaging myself a dancer and dreamer, whether taking Jonah, Brendan, Lukas or Jacob to the park or parking the car in a space much too small, whether nagging Patrick to change the oil or putting in 7 quarts in one day then being told they ALL had to be flushed out, I knew you were inside me, outside me, all around and laughing at my mistakes as much as I was. (Only now do I have the courage to tell Patrick because he can't do anything about it—pretty smart, huh?) I was notoriously extravagant yet could stiff a waitress if she didn't hustle. I guess I'm not too proud of that. I made a lot of money and never appreciated it like others did—I guess I'm not too proud of that either (but I always thought there'd be more) However, if I gave my word to do something for someone, they could take it to the bank; I guess that should count for something. I did forgive the people I loved but harbored resentments against those who wronged me. (Nothing too virtuous about that). Most of the time I was kind, and a real Christian: visiting the sick, helping the poor, the house bound, the prisoners. And I always worked exceptionally hard for all the kids and families entrusted to me through my job. I had a fantastic career. I was a trailblazer but that didn't come without a price and without a lot of long hours and exceptional work. There were times when I felt I shortchanged Patrick on the housekeeping and cooking end so I'll forego a halo. Besides, **What, after all, is a halo? It's only one more thing to keep clean.** *But can you forgive me the things I didn't do when I should have, and forgive me the things I did do when I shouldn't have? In the old <u>Hymn to God the Father</u> it says,*

Wilt thou forgive that sin, where I begun, which is my sin, though it were done before? Wilt thou forgive those sins through which I run and do them still, though still I do deplore? When thou hast done, thou hast not done, for I have more. Will thou forgive that sin, by which I' have won others to sin, and made my sin their door? Wilt thou forgive that sin which I did shun A year or two, but wallowed in a score? When thou hast done, thou hast not done. For I have more. (John Donne) *Now is a good time to wish I had more virtue than vice but, what can I do? I'll make you a deal: I'll sin no more if you will watch over the ones I leave behind. And will you hold dear the ones I held dear? God, how I will miss them. Although I can give up my life, it's harder than hell to give up my loves. I guess Dante knew what he was talking about when he said,* **"There is no greater sorrow than to recall a time of happiness in misery".**

I think about the riotous times I had on trips, at work, at home and know that I was happy. I think about walking into trees, driving in Florida, or just laughing my head off with Cassandra, and I know I was blessed. And John, How much joy he brought into my life even as I wanted to wring his neck. How alike we were and how proud of him I was. Please watch over them and assign special angels to them and their families. And although I can't be there to Grandmother anymore, please let them all know I'll be there in spirit and that I was the best Grandmother around; I shall never forget them nor, I know, shall they forget me

Let them know I grieve more for leaving them than they could possibly grieve for me.

This sphere is pretty hard to leave behind for if we didn't find happiness here, I learned it's..."Not in Utopia—subterranean fields—or some secreted island, heaven knows where! But in this very world, which is the world of all of us,--the place where, in the end we find our happiness, or not at all!"

Paraphrasing Nadine Stair, "If I had my life to live over, I'd dare to make more mistakes. I'd relax. I would limber up. I would be sillier than I have been this trip. I would take fewer things seriously. I would take more chances. I'd take more trips. I would climb more mountains and swim more rivers. I would eat more ice cream and less beans. I would perhaps have more actual troubles, but fewer imaginary ones. You see, I was one of those people who lived sensibly and sanely hour after hour, day after day. Oh, I've had my moments. But if I had it to do over again, I'd have more of them. In fact, I'd try to have nothing else. Just moments, one after another, instead of living so many years ahead of each day. If I could do it again, I'd travel lighter. If I had my life to live over, I would start barefoot earlier in the spring and stay that way later in the fall. I would go to more dances. I would ride more merry-go-rounds. I would pick more daisies". I would tell my family more not that I loved them because I did that every time I saw them but I'd tell them why and how much. Since I can't live my life over, will you try to do some of these things for all of us? And in the process, don't anticipate, just appreciate. Amen and goodbye, my loves.

EULOGIES FOR ALL KINDS OF PEOPLE AND ALL KINDS OF CIRCUMSTANCES

FOR AN ACADEMICIAN (SEE ALSO EDUCATOR, LIBRARIAN, PROFESSOR, TEACHER)

_____ loved knowledge and learning and lived her life accordingly. Although her knowledge was considerable, she was never condescending nor impatient with those of us who knew so little about so much. The hours and passion she spent accumulating wisdom and grace were hours that she dedicated quietly to you, the Source of all Knowledge. Ever inquisitive, ever curious about things not seen and dreams not dreamed, please let _____'s questions be answered as she is now able to turn the pages of your Book of Life and dream the dreams of the blessed. Grant her, O, Lord, eternal rest from facts and fictions nagging at her intellectually and the eternal peace which comes from finally knowing first-hand your love and your abundance...(if appropriate), through Christ our Lord...Amen.

FOR AN ACCOUNTANT
(SEE ALSO BANKER)

_____loved accounting for everything within his purview and will expect. You, I'm sure, to do a thorough and immediate audit of his time on earth. Since _____ was especially talented when it came to credits and debits, may You be generous as You credit him with a good life and forgetful when You come to the debit side of his ledger. Although our hours on this planet are few, _____ tried to make every minute count because he knew that time is the only currency which—once spent—can never be recovered nor spent again. _____ accumulated a lot of our interest as he watched over our books with careful attention to detail, enriching our lives in ways that multiplied our resources and saved us time. Although it may not all be on the spreadsheet before You, if you check our entries, You'll see that this is one person upon whom we could always count.

FOR AN ACTOR/ACTRESS (SEE ALSO MODEL, MUSCIAN)

Dear Lord,

Wasn't it Shakespeare who said, "All the world's a stage and all the men and women merely players.... they have their exits and their entrances, and each, in his time plays many parts? Well, _____ certainly played many parts and played them well. Although known and remembered best, perhaps, for her role in _____, those of us who knew and loved her appreciated the fact that she never acted when it came to loving us. She worked hard at her craft but never forgot the source of her talent and never felt she was so good that she didn't need to keep improving. Her energy was a source of inspiration for all who knew her and her ability to portray the range of human emotions and characters was something to be envied. Of course, we would much rather see her make another entrance today rather than this final exit but know that You will insure the Grandest Entrance of all time as you welcome her into your cast of billions. Although her time with us was much too brief, we are comforted by the fact that she will now be a Star for all eternity.

FOR AN ADMINISTRATOR
(SEE ALSO BOSS, CEO/CFO)

_____ liked things to work smoothly in all aspects of his life. But he never sacrificed compassion for competency nor friendship for frenzy. He was organized and efficient and inspired his subordinates to buy into his vision so we/they were all moving in the same direction. Attention to detail was one of his many strengths but so was his attention to people. By working side by side and being highly visible, he let us/them know what we/they were doing was worth the effort. He had a way of recognizing and rewarding talent and had a talent for downplaying his role in the company's joint success. Productivity and positive staff morale were just two of the legacies he leaves behind. We assume you needed someone pretty badly up there to run a new division when you took him from us, and we certainly would serve as a reference on his overall job performance. But, if You could, please let him do the annual evaluations of those he left behind so we'll be sure we can join him years from now in Your office, on the production line, or at one of Your assemblies.

FOR AN ADOPTED CHILD (SEE ALSO CHILD, DAUGHTER, INFANT, SON)

Dear Lord,

How we loved him! And how we loved You for gifting us with his life! (We believe St. Joseph knew what it was like to have a Son that was his by gift rather than genetic formula and we ask for his support during these days of our loss). It is said when you bury a parent, you bury the past but when you bury a child, you bury the future. His future looked so bright and ours, by just having him in our lives, looked so promising. Now all we can look forward to are tears and heartache. Please help us remember the good times and remember that his was a life complete, rather than a life terminated. Although we chose _____, it seemed more often than not, he chose us. From the day we brought him home, there was something about him that seemed to fit. We dreamed his dreams, bandaged his bumps, assuaged his broken heart, and lit up every time he smiled at us sitting in the wings or in the grandstands cheering him on. We know he was on loan—as all children are—but it seems like we had him such a short period of time. Please help us get through the pain so we can once again embrace the joy that was ours from the moment we met this angel on earth. If hugs can reach him in heaven, please make sure new "parents" or angels lavish him with the same love he takes with him to his new home. We would not have willingly left him on Your doorstep but trust that You'll take him into your hearth and your heart and let him know, once again, he was wanted very, very much. "No flesh of my flesh nor bone of my bone, but still miraculously my own. Never forget for a single minute, you didn't grow under my heart—but in it". (Anonymous.)

FOR AN ADOPTED PARENT (SEE ALSO FATHER, MOTHER, GRAND/PARENT)

Dear Lord,

I called her Mom (him Dad) because in every way—except biologically—that's what she was to me. Although I was born to someone else, she was the one meant to hold me, comfort me, cuddle me, guide me, and watch me grow. Each year as I sprouted another inch or two on the wall chart, it seemed my love for my adopted Mom (or Dad) grew a hundred fold. My life could have been bleak or less fulfilled, but Mom (or Dad) showered me with love and wisdom and grace and let me know that I was wanted and wished for by them from the time of my existence. And although they said they chose me, I really chose them. If I had it all to do over again, I would choose them still. For they have been the stars in the firmament of my heaven, my touchstone, my heart's music, and home to all my needs and desires. They have dressed me in love, sheltered me in hope, and bathed me in faith that life will be as good to me as they have been. What could have been tragic was a blessing years ago and, I pray, what I see as tragic today—losing Mom (or Dad)—is also a prelude to a better life that we'll adopt together in eternity. Amen.

FOR AN ANIMAL LOVER

Dear Lord,

You Who love all creatures great and small, please take special note today of this person entering your kingdom. _____ was an animal lover with a magnetism that attracted animals and held their devotion for most of her life. Solicitous of their health and well-being, she would often go miles out of her way to make sure they received food, shelter, and comfort as needed. People in the neighborhood referred to her as the "Pied Piper of Pets" because the minute she came into view, dogs would cross the street to get stroked or fed something from her pocket. And it wasn't uncommon to see squirrels and raccoons eating out of her hand in the woods. She was equally good with horses who would nuzzle her as she approached. It seemed she always had treats and was such a gentle soul that she could reassure even the most frightened or wounded animal to trust her. Please keep in mind her gentleness and goodness of spirit and reassure her if she's frightened today that she can trust You to look after her and those she leaves behind as we lay her to rest. Amen.

FOR AN ANTIQUE DEALER

Dear Lord,

As a lover of antiquities and a historian of "pieces", _____ has put great stock in things that are precious and part of the past. She was precious to us and now must become part of our past as You welcome her into Your House. Please tolerate her snooping around for awhile to see what collectibles You have accumulated over the centuries. Certainly, in a manner of speaking, with all the potential antiques, _____ will think she's died and "gone to heaven". _____ recognized that the rareness of an item was enhanced by its condition and, as rare as she was, we hope you'll see her condition as one worthy of prizing among your greatest "pieces". Cognizant of rare stones and jewelry, connoisseur of estates, and assessor of what was to be valued over the ages, we trust that you will see her as more valuable than a Hope Diamond or a priceless antique to be added to your eternal estate. She was a collector of people, Lord, let us who are left behind value the memories as much as the memorabilia she left behind.

FOR AN ARTIST

Dear Lord,

An artist finds beauty in strange places, living a life with a different set of glasses than those worn by more ordinary folk, seeing color when the rest of us see simple gray. As you welcome _____ into your Kingdom, please accommodate his perspective and allow for a little idiosyncrasy and artistic temperament from time to time. We probably all fell short of his definition of beauty but he imbued us with a reverence for it and made us want to stretch our horizons to feed our hungry souls. Please be compassionate about his passion and the path he trod as a result of his insatiable need to find light in darkness, melody in static, and harmony in chaos. On Your eternal canvas, please allow him the space and material to imprint his style for those of us who come after. Help him to find the wonderful Kaleidoscope of your Heaven for which he searched unceasingly all the days of his life. And accept his art as an expression of your infinite majesty and magnificence as he takes up his palette on another plane for now and forever.

***Rejoice** by Bridges (1844-1930)*

"Rejoice ye dead, where'er your spirits dwell,
Rejoice that yet on earth your fame is bright,
And that your names, remembered day and night,
Live on the lips of those who love you well.

FOR AN ASTROLOGIST (SEE PILOT, ALSO *CELESTIAL FLIGHT* AT END OF BOOK)

We are burying a dear person today; one who believed in celestial powers and consulted horoscopes for everything from soup to nuts. She looked to the Zodiac for guidance and was willing to give freely of her special insights. She was always there for us as she checked the charts, studied the tides and their effect on the moon, and listened to her inner compass. Although she felt a special connection to things spiritual and paraphysical, some of us didn't share her belief or her perspicacity, so we mourn her loss without the kind of perspective she might have been able to impart. Please watch over her as she studies the stars "up close and personal" now and forever, amen

Go placidly amid the noise and haste, and remember what peace there may be in silence. As far a possible, without surrender, be on good terms with all persons. Speak your truth quietly and clearly; and listen to others, even the dull and ignorant; they, too, have their story. Avoid loud and aggressive persons; they are vexations to the spirit. If you compare yourself with others,, you may become vain and bitter; for always there will be greater and lesser persons than yourself. Enjoy your achievements as well as your plans. Keep interested in your own career, however, humble; it is a real possession in the changing fortunes of time. Exercise caution in your business affairs; for the world is full of trickery. But let this not blind you to what virtue there is; many persons strive for high ideals; and everywhere life is full of heroism.

Be yourself. Especially, do not feign affection. Neither be cynical about love; for in the face of all aridity and disenchantment it is perennial as the grass. Take kindly the council of the years, gracefully surrendering the things of youth. Nurture strength of spirit to shield you in sudden misfortune. But do not distress yourself with imaginings. Many fears are born of fatigue and loneliness. Beyond a wholesale discipline, be gentle with yourself. You are a child of the universe, no less than the trees and the stars; you have a right to be here. And whether or not it is clear to you, no doubt the universe is unfolding as it should. Therefore be at peace with God, whatever you conceive Him to be, and whatever your labors and aspirations, in the noisy confusion of life keep peace with your soul. With all its sham, drudgery and broken dreams, it is still a beautiful world. Be careful. Strive to be happy.

FOR AN ASTRONAUT

It has been said jokingly that the only reason they allowed females to become astronauts was because they weren't afraid to ask directions but we know there were many other, more serious, reasons. Like courage, intelligence, sensitivity, and perseverance. As we gather today to pay our respects to _____, we call to mind those very qualities. She was a leader whether on the ground or out in space, she was a supporter of her teammates and her life mates, she was dependable, diligent, and determined to do well as she soared above our planet and reached, literally, for the stars. She is among the stars today, we are sure. She's tough, she's a trailblazer, and she's probably setting up a comfortable space station to make room for us when it's time for our souls to take similar flight. And fortunately, she'll be there to give directions if we lose our way. May she continue to rise in your eyes beyond the stature she has earned here in ours. Amen.

FOR AN ATHEIST

We come today to bury someone who didn't believe in God nor a life after death. Yet he was a good man. We want to acknowledge his life as he lived it. Although he professed no belief in a God, he lived a godly life, never hurting someone deliberately, always treating fellow human beings with respect and, yes, even a kind of reverence. _____ was dependable, reliable, and shared his time and talent with us. As was said of Robert Ingersoll, the *great agnostic*, "he died yesterday. Perhaps he knows better now." As we say goodbye, we pray that his beliefs won't matter as much as his behavior toward fellow human beings and, in Your eyes, will make his short time on earth justification enough for his life, for, "No man is an island, entire of its self; every man is a piece of the continent, a part of the main; if a clod be washed away from the sea, Europe is the less, as well as a promontory were, as well as if a manor of thy friends or of thine own were; any man's death diminishes me, because I am involved in Mankind... (Donne, Meditation, XVII)

FOR AN ATHLETE (SEE ALSO JOGGER)

The race goes to the swiftest and _____ was, indeed, swift. He worked hard at being fit and was competitive from a very early age. His sports were exceedingly important to him and he showed us how to balance that love with other loves of his life. He used his body as an instrument, fine tuning it, and taking care of it so he could always expect top performance. Never measuring his performance against others but only against his own record, he demonstrated an unusual commitment to excellence. May we, too, treat our bodies and our achievements with the same respect and recognition that they are to be used for your honor and glory and are just one of your gifts to us in this life.

_____ died as he lived, in good shape, mentally and physically still eager to run the race. In his death he has broken all of the previous records of his life, winning laurels and rest, finally, for all eternity.

FOR AN AUNT

Aunt _____ was a family member who helped us come together on many occasions to keep us connected. She was a dear sister to our father/mother, doting on us when we were young, hovering over us as we grew. She was a surrogate parent, counseling, cajoling, kidding, and loving us. She never played favorites but only the games that would make us happy. She seemed young forever yet wiser than her years; take her into Your bosom and watch over her until we meet again. Amen.

FOR AN AUTHOR

You who are the Author of Life, lover of peace and concord, in knowledge of whom standeth our eternal life, whose service is perfect freedom; Defend us thy humble servants in all assaults of our enemies and welcome _____, an author of words and bearer of exceptional talent. Although willing to share his wisdom and knowledge with us, he knew that an author who speaks about his own books is almost as bad as a mother who talks about nothing but her own children. He read a lot into life and helped us see the world through his eyes many times. As said about translating Homer, he knew the three essential qualities of being an author and adhered to them throughout his life: 1) that he be eminently rapid; 2) that he be eminently plain and direct both in the evolution of thought and in the expression of if; and 3) that he be eminently noble. _____ exemplified these qualities as well as many others that endeared him to us. Although a man of many words, he made us feel as though we, too, were capable of deep and noble thought in everyday conversation. May he find in our feeble words the depth of respect and affection we had for him and may his works live forever.

Rejoice by Bridges (1844-1930)

**"Rejoice ye dead, where'er your spirits dwell,
Rejoice that yet on earth your fame is bright,
And that your names, remembered day and night,
Live on the lips of those who love you well.**

FOR A BABY (SEE ALSO ADOPTED/CHILD, INFANT

Dear Lord,

As we struggle with a loss which rips apart our hearts today, help us find strength that is many times greater than the little body we hold so close. Help us heal for we know that nothing hurts as much as this. Although _____ was tiny, her impact on our lives was monumental. She lit our doorways and made the fairies sing. It was as if she knew Peter Pan's claim that when the first baby laughed for the first time, the laughter broke into a thousand pieces and became fairies with all their skipping about. Lord, help remind us about the fairies when we get really low in the days to come. _____ already reminded us of how close heaven can be. It is said when you lose a parent, you bury the past but when you lose a child, you bury the future. Right now it's hard to imagine a future worth living without _____ but we must not only imagine it; we must begin to live it from this moment on. We will need your help and the help of our family and friends. Please let them know that it's not only okay to talk about our loss—it's essential—if we're ever going to get past this pain. And help us watch over our other children as we all go through the work of grieving so they, too, can not only "keep the faith" but someday understand the reason for such heartache. Perhaps You just needed some magic laughter up there Yourself.

FOR A BAKER

How sweet it was to have shared a life with _____ _____. The aromas and memories triggered over the years by her labors are some of our best. We could always get a rise out of her by buttering her up or asking for dough. We used to tease her by saying she was a pretty smart cookie but she had the twinkle that seems common to bakers the world over; it was as though making edibles and sweets was the way she said she loved us. Giving us our daily bread and just desserts reminded us of her warmth and reassurances. Please take good care of her; make sure she can have her cake and eat it too. She deserves all the treats in store for someone who has led a good, sweet, life.

FOR A BANKER (SEE ALSO ACCOUNTANT)

Dear Lord,

Money was the tool with which _____ _____ passed his day but was not the important currency of his heart. His treasure lay in his family and friends and everything else was secondary. Although he was reliable, dependable, somewhat conservative, and rock solid in his career, _____ was funny, warm, and engaging after hours. His serious banker's face stayed at the bank, while the husband's and father's faces were the ones he wore home. He taught many to marshal resources and invest wisely but the biggest lesson we all learned from him was "where the heart is, there the treasure is also". As he puts down the coins of this life, please help him quickly find gold and something he can bank on in the next.

FOR A BASEBALL FAN OR PLAYER

Dear Lord,

It looks like this is _____'s final inning at bat. Although his score may not be that impressive in Your league, we felt he was a real player and wanted him on our roster regardless of the opposition. He believed that practice is what makes you perfect and spent hours honing his skills. He threw himself into life, caught his own mistakes, and was always making a pitch for others. As he takes his place in your field, please watch over him and give him a lot of "at bats" since he worked hard here on earth to deserve them. He ran the bases, fielded the grounders, and cheered his teammates on. Now that he has hit the final home run we won't see him rounding your bases but have gathered here to cheer him on just the same.

FOR A BACHELOR/BACHELORETTE

Dear Lord,

As we say farewell to one who has lived his life well, we want to acknowledge how important _____ _____'s style of life was to him. Although we probably hounded him too often to find someone to marry, it's obvious in retrospect that he made the right choice in staying single. He had so much to share with so many, he wouldn't have had time to do justice to all his interests if he had committed to only one person forever. We now commit this singular soul to your good keeping knowing that'll he'll be looked after in a manner to which he will become eternally accustomed.

FOR A BOARD MEMBER

Dear Lord,

He liked to pound the gavel but I think it was just to make sure everyone got their chance to voice their opinion. He was fair, effective, and concerned about this organization. Please help him to conduct himself and his celestial meetings with as much enthusiasm and aplomb as he mustered here on earth.

FOR A BOAT ENTHUSIAST
(SEE ALSO SAILOR)

_____ loved the water in almost any form and many of our happiest memories of him are those we recall when he was behind his prow, making waves and having a "swell" time. He showed the same courtesy on the water as he did on land and was a real gentleman. He exemplified the wisdom of **Desiderada,**

Be yourself....Take kindly the council of years, gracefully surrendering the things of youth. Nurture strength of spirit to shield you in sudden misfortune. But do not distress yourself with imaginings. Many fears are born of fatigue and loneliness. Beyond a wholesome discipline, be gentle with yourself. You are a child of the Universe, no less than the trees and the stars; you have a right to be here. And whether or not it is clear to you, no doubt the Universe is unfolding as it should. Therefore, be at peace with God, whatever you conceive him to be, and whatever your labors and aspirations, in the noisy confusion of life, keep peace with your soul." He knew "with all its sham, drudgery, and broken dreams, it is still a beautiful world" and was always able—especially when on his boat—to find contentment May he sail into heaven placidly amid the noise and haste of the world he leaves behind.

FOR A BOSS (SEE ALSO ADMINISTRATOR, CEO/CFO)

In life, few people make good bosses. _____ _____ was such a woman. She cared about her workers and they, in turn, helped turn her division into a top performer. She had a sense of humor and a sense of timing that let us know when we could work hard and when we could play just as hard. She knew us as individuals and encouraged our growth both on and outside of the job. She was familiar with our familial needs and helped us meet all our obligations without feeling guilty if we had to modify our schedules. To her, our performance not our punctuality was the standard by which she measured us. May she be measured in the same fashion. Amen.

FOR A BROTHER

Dear Lord,

Brothers are things you grow up with and sometimes they're not all that pleasant. But this brother was dear from the moment he entered my life. Since my affection for him makes the English alphabet inadequate, I thought I'd quote (**secular**) from an old English author, Cavell, "By many lands and over many a wave I come, my brother, to your piteous grave, to bring you the last offering in death and o'er dumb dust expend an idle breath. For fate has torn your living self from me, and snatched you, brother, O, how cruelly! Yet take these gifts, brought as our fathers bade for sorrow's tribute to the passing shade; A brother's tears have wet them o'er and o'er; and so, my brother, hail, and farewell, evermore!" _____ lived his life according to his own drummer at times but also in philosophical harmony with the advice from the **Desiderada**: Be yourself....Take kindly the council of years, gracefully surrendering the things of youth. Nurture strength of spirit to shield you in sudden misfortune. But do not distress yourself with imaginings. Many fears are born of fatigue and loneliness. Beyond a wholesome discipline, be gentle with yourself. You are a child of the Universe, no less than the trees and the stars; you have a right to be here. And whether or not it is clear to you, no doubt the Universe is unfolding as it should. Therefore, be at peace with God, whatever you conceive him to be, and whatever your labors and aspirations, in the noisy confusion of life, keep peace with your soul." He knew "with all its sham, drudgery, and broken dreams, it is still a beautiful world". He and his philosophy of life will be missed by those he loved. (*religious*) "Forasmuch as it has pleased Almighty God of his great mercy to take unto himself the soul of our dear brother here departed, we therefore commit his body to the ground; earth to earth, ashes to ashes, dust to dust; in sure and certain hope of the Resurrection to eternal life, through our Lord Jesus Christ; who shall change our vile body, that it may be like unto his glorious body, according to the mighty working whereby he is able to subdue all things to himself". Amen.

BUILDER

Dear Lord,

St. Joseph was a carpenter and made that profession noble for the ages. _____ treated his craft with almost the same reverence. As an old philosopher once said, "when we build, let us think we build forever". I think _____ thought just that, so committed to perfection and beauty was he. In chapter 5 of the *Lamp of Life*, it is written "I believe the right question to ask respecting any ornament is simply this: was it done with enjoyment? Was the builder happy with it?" those of us who knew _____ _____ could honestly say, "yes" he loved what he was doing and what he was doing day in and day out was expressing that love of beauty and that pride that comes from knowing you've done your best. Lord, take him into your heavenly kingdom and let him know if you need any repairs; it'll keep him busy as he waits for the ones he left behind.

FOR A BUSINESS ASSOCIATE (SEE ALSO BOSS, CEO/CFO, CO-WORKER)

Dear Lord,

Business has lost a great leader today. Although the Dow Jones Average may not reflect it, we know we're not burying an average guy. _____ worked hard and made sure that his work was without reproach. In an age where planned obsolescence is taken for granted, he could have put the Maytag Repair Man out of business for he took great pride in his tasks and exemplified the kind of worker we would all love to have by our side.

(See below.)

FOR A BUSINESSMAN/ WOMAN (SEE BUSINESS ASSOCIATE, BOSS, CEO/CFO)

Dear Lord,

The Wall Street Journal may not have put _____ _____'s passing on its front page but it's front page news to us because of its impact on our lives. Please help us enjoy the memories of all his accomplishments and forget the pain of losing him. He brought his company to the summit almost single-handedly. And although we know for him the bottom line was very important, we also know that his family, friends and co-workers were the first considerations whenever he studied the ledger of his life. Please help us in his passing and recognize as you greet him that he left big shoes to fill so we'll all need your support over the next several months as we adjust to the loss of someone of his stature.

FOR A BUSDRIVER

Dear Lord,

_____ already had her ticket punched for a trip to the end of the line. Help her speed into heaven without having to stop for railroad tracks and speed bumps along the way. She was patient with her passengers, never demanding an excessive toll and always delivering them safely to their destination. Cheerfully greeting them, she kept her eye on their safety as she glimpsed life through her rear view mirror. Help her now to lay on the horn as she approaches the pearly gates and grant her admittance to your heavenly kingdom.

FOR A CADDIE

_____ willingly carried the burden of others, championing their cause and keeping their score so they could concentrate on the game at hand. Today we bear tribute to such a humble man and hope someone will now carry his burdens for all eternity. **Come unto me all that labour and are heavy laden, and I will give you rest. Take my yoke upon you and learn of me; for I am meek and lowly in heart; and you shall find rest unto your souls. For my yoke is easy and my burden is light. (St. Matthew 28. Amen.)**

FOR A CARPENTER (SEE ALSO BUILDER)

At times it seems like being a carpenter has been one of the noblest professions known to man. Not only was St. Joseph the prototype for a man who worked with his hands while nurturing with his soul, but he also stood for fatherhood and the family provider. May _____ bask in the same kind of status in your heavenly kingdom. He spent his days on earth building habitats, may he spend eternity in heaven repairing your many mansions.

FOR A CASHIER

_____ must have gotten so tired dealing with irate customers, irresponsible co-workers, and penny after penny after penny that perhaps you took her just so she wouldn't have to make change one more time. Although her job would have challenged the most patient of us, she seldom complained. Instead she smiled and treated the customer as she herself would want to be treated. Maybe that's the legacy she leaves behind. Instead of cashing out, we should realize she has cashed in and traded all those moments for reward in the great store above.

FOR A CELEBRITY (SEE ALSO ACTOR, ARTIST, AUTHOR)

Dear Lord,

Although fame is fleeting, your love is constant. Help us remember _____ not for her fame but for her fidelity to friends and family. Not for her beauty (for we know beauty is nature's way of bragging, not hers), but for her humility. Help us remember that she rose to stardom yet handled it well. She was able to "keep her head while others about her were losing theirs". She remained confident, compassionate and strong. Help the ones who loved her most to cope with this great loss.

***Rejoice** by Bridges (1844-1930)*

**"Rejoice ye dead, where'er your spirits dwell,
Rejoice that yet on earth your fame is bright,
And that your names, remembered day and night,
Live on the lips of those who love you well.**

FOR A CEO/CFO (ALSO SEE BOSS, ADMINISTRATOR, CO-WORKER)

Although it would have been easy for _____ _____ to lose the common touch, she never did. She worked hard and showed those around her how to have high standards without standing on the backs of others. She outperformed most of us yet never acted like she thought she was any better. She loved to work and made us love it too. Help those she leaves behind for the absence of such a bright star will leave a real vacuum for a very long time.

FOR A CHARACTER (SEE ALSO PRACTICAL JOKER)

We promised _____ we wouldn't cry but rather we would come together to celebrate her life and laughter. This is one person who knew how to live! _____ taught us that you don't have to be handed all the things the world says you need to be happy, you simply need to adjust your attitude so that happiness can't help but trip over you. We will miss _____ because there wasn't a day that she didn't make us see things with a different—and delightful—perspective. It's hard to imagine being able to laugh without her around but I know she'd agree with the old saying, "Better by far that you should forget and smile than that you should remember and be sad." Help us try not to be sad as we say goodbye and godspeed.

FOR A CHILD (SEE ALSO INFANT, ADOPTED CHILD, BABY)

Dear Lord,

We know the lord giveth and the lord taketh away. We just didn't expect it to be so soon or at such a high cost. But we also know that even though Isaiah claims a woman could forget her sucking child that she might not have compassion on the son of her womb, we know that you will not forget us. The Bible tells us "He shall feed his block like a shepherd; he shall gather the lambs with his arm and carry them in his bosom and shall gently lead those that are with young.... back home". Please carry this child safely back to your bosom. The hours/days/years we spent watching over him will seem so few in comparison to the hours/days/years now looming ahead of us. We felt like Edna St. Vincent Milllaly that "Childhood is not from birth to a certain age and at a certain age the child is grown, and puts away childish things. Childhood is the kingdom where nobody dies. Nobody that matters, that is". Why did _____'s childhood have to end with his/her own death? Help us remember the joy in his small discoveries, the excitement in his first achievements, and the ecstasy that was ours when we simply could rock him to sleep in our arms. Help us to accept this loss as part of your divine plan and help us guide his siblings from the fear that they, too, may die too soon. Let our families and friends know we need to talk about _____ in order to cope with our loss, manage our grief, and get on with our lives. Watch over the young at play and please give us the grace, perspective, and compassion to once again care about other children. Amen.

FOR A CITY OFFICIAL

So many times _____ toiled with no recognition and tangible rewards. So many times he put in the extra hours and the extra effort when no one was looking. In his steady and humble service, he taught us that one can serve nobly and consistently and be respected for it by others. May his influence continue to be a part of the city he loved so that when he looks over us, he sees a proliferation of all his efforts and progress that is nothing short of miraculous as we strive to make his having passed this way but once something that will effect city residences now and in future years to come. Amen.

FOR A CLERIC (SEE ALSO, MINISTER, PRIEST, RABBI)

Dear Lord,

At church, with meek and unaffected grace, his looks adorn'd the venerable place; truth from his lips prevail'd with double sway, and fools, who came to scoff, remain'd to pray. (Goldsmith, 1730-74) **God be in my head**...And in my understanding...God be in my eyes...And in my looking...God be in my mouth...And in my speaking...God be in my heart...And in my thinking...God be at my end...And at my departing. (Sarum Missal). We're so used to him saying words over bodies or being first to light lanterns over the grave, please give us grace and grasp of English to do it right for him.

May _____ rest in eternal peace and quiet away from long sermons and boring homilies. Away from people who always wanted free advice and a shoulder to lean on. And may he find the rewards as promised people whose lives were reflections of you; may he know eternal love and celestial friendship to make up for the loneliness that often accompanied him in his relentless pursuit of peace for his fellow men and women on earth. Amen.

FOR A COACH

Dear Lord,

He knew when You, the Great Scorer, came to write against his name that you would mark not that he won or lost but how he taught his athletes to play the game...of life.

We come together to honor a man (woman) who was more than just a coach. How many times did our sons and daughters come home and say "But Coach says to do it this way..." _____ was such a stickler for fundamentals that he had a rare ability to balance those requisite skills with fun so that kids could learn yet love the game. His dignity and integrity on the field helped all of us remember that we were there for sportsmanship first. May he take his many skills into your Kingdom and receive the same kind of respect, patience and support that he displayed day in and day out while here on earth.

FOR A COMPUTER TECHNICIAN

Although we may not have understood everything _____ did, we do know that he loved it and was among the best in the field. It was wonderful to see him speaking to the computer as though it was an instrument simply in need of tuning. He exemplified knowledge and a self-respect that broached little disagreement. He kept current and yet was willing to spend hours and hours explaining the ins and outs of how our computer worked so we could benefit from his knowledge. He never made us feel stupid and for that alone we'll be eternally grateful. Help us to say goodbye in a language he'll understand and give him all the gigabits he requires, now and forever. Amen.

FOR A CONNOISSEUR

_____ knew the fine art of discrimination when it came to many things in life. Although she mastered the differences between wine, she also took on many challenges to use her deep well of knowledge. She enjoyed her work and her life and left behind many friends who felt they had exquisite taste because they had her at the top of every list.

FOR A CONSERVATIONALIST (SEE ALSO ANIMAL LOVER, GARDENER),

_____ loved nature in its entirety and took great pleasure in the wealth of the fields and the vastness of your space in which to draw a beautiful world. Although _____ would not have considered herself a gardener, these thoughts come to mind, "the poetry of earth is never dead; When all the birds are faint with the hot sun, and hide in cooling trees, a voice will run from hedge to hedge about the new mown lawn" (*On the Grasshopper and Cricket* by Keats). *As Thomas Moore said in 1842,* ***No, the heart that has truly lov'd never forgets, But as truly loves on to the close, As the sunflower turns on her god, when he sets, the same look which she turn'd when he rose.*** *This sphere is pretty hard to leave behind for if we didn't find happiness here, I learned it's..."Not in Utopia—subterranean fields—or some secreted island, heaven knows where! But in this very world, which is the world of all of us,--the place where, in the end we find our happiness, or not at all!"*

FOR A CONSTRUCTION WORKER (SEE ALSO CARPENTER, BUILDER)

DEAR LORD,

_____ was happiest when working and because of that made an excellent provider for his family. An old philosopher once said, "When we build, let us think we build forever". I think _____ _____ thought just that, so committed to perfection and beauty was he. In chapter 5 of the *Lamp of Life*, it is written "I believe the right question to ask respecting any ornament is simply this: was it done with enjoyment? was the builder happy with it?". Those of us who knew _____ could honestly say, "yes" he loved what he was doing. He made of the lumber of his life not a tavern but a tabernacle; may we do likewise in ours.

FOR A COOK/CHEF (SEE ALSO BAKER, RESTRAUTEUR)

Dear Lord,

We have been treated well by _____. Never did he make us feel if we were alone that we should be rushed out to make room for more customers and whenever he ran out of the daily specials, he'd cook something up just for us. He reminded us of an old fashioned hotelier and saw his place of business as a home away from home for his friends. An Earl in 1860 said, "We may live without poetry, music or art; We may live without conscience, and live without heart; We may live without friends, we may live without books; But civilized man cannot live without cooks". May you make him feel as welcomed as he always made us feel—and that's anything but a "short order", Lord.

"Since ev'ry man who lives in born to die, And none can boast sincere felicity, With equal mind, what happens, let us bear, Nor joy nor grieve too much for things beyond our care. Like pilgrims to th' appointed place we tend; The world's an inn, and death the journey's end. John Dryden (1631-1700)

FOR A COSMETOLOGIST/ NAIL TECHNICIAN

Dear Lord,

Thanks to people like _____ the men and women of this world are better off, coifed, buffed and polished and set to go upon their daily personal and professional errands. How many confidences _____ kept, how many words of encouragement over a sink, a rinse, and an acrylic did she minister to us the tired, the dragged-in, dragged out customer! She was like a friend in whom we found refuge; a collector of secrets we could trust. Take good and loving care of your servant, Lord; she sure took good care of us.

FOR A COUSIN

Dear Lord,

Related by blood but bound by interests, _____ _____ was the kind of friend everyone should have but few do. Although we socialized from time to time because of family connections, we really connected emotionally and would have made it a point to stay close regardless, for absence is to love what wind is to fire; it extinguishes the small, it enkindles the great. Bussy-Rabutin, (1693). Ours was (was not) the kind of association that came together only for funerals and weddings; rather it was an association built on love, trust, and enjoyment of each others' gifts S/he will be missed.

FOR A CO-WORKER (SEE ALSO BUSINESS ASSOCIATE)

Dear Lord,

We have spent many hours with _____ _____ and appreciated her attention to detail, her willingness to contribute to the team effort and her sincere concern for others. We come to say farewell today around a water cooler of sorts as we wish her "God speed". We wanted her to take with her to her next place of business the best wishes of those with whom she toiled. She was an example to our department of industriousness, dependability, and commitment. Yet she was also remarkably approachable and perceptive. She knew when we needed time alone and when we needed a pat on the back. She encouraged us along our way, please do the same for her.

FOR A CRAFTSMAN

Dear Lord,

The more difficult the craft, the more demanding standards _____ had for herself. We used to kid her that she spent so much time and money on her art that she'd have to charge a thousand dollars for each piece just so she'd break even! She loved putzing around and had an eye for beauty that sometimes took our breath away. Her craft was one of the ways she expressed herself to the world and was, therefore, something we'll value beyond her years on earth. All the craft shows and art fairs she forced us to attend just reinforced her determination to constantly improve. Let us carry away from here that same kind of resolve as we go about making the remainders of our lives works of art.

FOR A CRANKY PERSON

Dear Lord,

_____ was not the most cheerful soul and no doubt will find something in this service to complain about but, ironically, that constant was one of the things about _____ we hold most dear. Although _____ was often gruff and complaining, those of us who knew him well knew that inside he was a marshmallow just wanting to be loved. Forgive him his pettiness and see instead the larger picture whereby he tried to be a perfectionist and was simply attempting to help others measure up to his version of the perfect life. We will strive to become the kind of people he felt we should be as we seek your kingdom in the hereafter.

FOR A CROSSING GUARD

Dear Lord,

Almost like St. Christopher, _____ was a patron saint of the school children who crossed at her corner every day. She knew them by name, and often would stop traffic in order to ensure their safety. She was as dedicated as the mail man: Neither snow, nor hail, nor sleet, nor rain would keep her from her appointed post. Help her cross over to your kingdom as we on earth sound the horns for her one last time.

FOR A CUSTODIAN/ ENVIRONMENT ENGINEER

Dear Lord,

Keep it clean seemed to be _____'s refrain. Garbage in, garbage out held special meaning for him. Working in a job that most of us took for granted but would never undertake ourselves, _____ brought dignity to a profession that's often maligned. Help us to justly commemorate his contributions to our high standard of living and recognize him for the clean person he was. Picking up after others is not an easy task; please give him a squad of angels who will clean up any messes he left behind so he can be seated immediately at your right hand for now and all eternity. Amen.

FOR A DANCER

Dear Lord,

How lightly she danced through life and how she graced our lives with rhythms that only she could hear. She seemed almost ephemeral as she moved from one stage in her life to another; almost a spirit as she hovered over the good times and added beauty to the bad. She loved to sway to her own tunes yet life for her seemed a symphony that we could hear snatches of whenever she drew close. We remember her style, her verve, her energy, her passion. Please, Lord, do the same. For she died as she lived: with grace enough for all of us.

FOR A DAUGHTER (SEE ALSO, BABY, ADOPTED CHILD, CHILD, INFANT)

Dear Lord,
Where and how do I begin to tell these people of the story of my love. How can I give up a bosom buddy, a guiding light, the light of my life? How can I ever laugh again when every time I do it will break into a thousand pieces of broken heart as I remember how we giggled, laughed, and sometimes even roared as we talked and reminisced long into the nights. How can I possibly bear such a burden and still go on living a life that now seems to have so little meaning? As Mark Twain said upon the death of his daughter, "It is one of the mysteries of our nature that a man, all unprepared, can receive a thunderstroke like that and live." Please help me to remember her as she was in the September of her years—when grass was green and grain was yellow; and when no one wept except the willow. I know that without a hurt, our hearts are hollow but, Lord, mine feels down right wooden. Please let her know often that she was loved for the short time she was on loan to us and please give us the peace of mind that comes eventually from knowing that she never felt alone in her pain because she knew we'd "go to the ends of the earth" for her. And please, like Demeter with Persephone, let us know that when spring returns it's only because our daughter has come back to be at our side as we continue through our own vale of tears.

"For winter's rains and ruins are over, And all the season of snows and sins: The days dividing lover and lover, The light that loses, the night that wins; And time remembered is grief forgotten, And frosts are slain and flowers begotten, And in green underwood and cover Blossom by blossom the spring begins...Before the beginning of years came to the making of man Time with a gift of tears, Grief with a glass that ran...Strength without hands to smite, Love that endures for a breath; Night, the shadow of light, And Life, the shadow of death....From too much love of living, From hope and fear set free, We thank with brief thanksgiving Whatever gods may be..." Please watch over her, Lord, she's used to being loved.

FOR A DIRECTOR OF A NON-PROFIT

dear lord,

_____ gave her waking hours to a calling that meant little in money but much in the way of the intangibles—like helping others who were less fortunate. St. Peter tells us that **Charity shall cover the multitude of sins** so we know we don't need to seek your pardon for any of her shortcomings today but , rather, we wanted to celebrate the joy that was hers as she gave so unselfishly of her time and talent to feed, clothe, and shelter the poor. As the lord reminds us: Inasmuch as ye have done it unto one of the least of these my brethren, ye have done it unto me. For I was hungred and ye gave me meat; I was thirsty and ye gave me drink; I was a stranger and ye took me in; naked and ye clothed me; I was sick and ye visited me; I was in prison and you came to me. Lord, recognize that _____ gave her life to the unfortunate. Please take her in and shelter, feed and clothe her in your heavenly garments now and forever. Amen.

FOR A DIVORCEE/DIVORCED PERSON (SEE ALSO ESTRANGED FAMILY MEMBER)

Dear Lord,

Please help the family of _____ so recently divided. Although no longer part of a marital union, we consider _____ still family and bring our grief to his graveside as we acknowledge how much we loved him and how much we missed him before he was taken away by you. Our hearts are still suffering from the first departure, help us gird ourselves for this permanent one. Help, especially, anyone who felt guilty about his dissolved marriage and keep his children safe from harm. Not every marriage works out but his efforts were steady and sincere, even if unsuccessful. Let us acknowledge that he will always retain a special place in our hearts although he had left our homes some time ago.

FOR A DOCTOR

Dear Lord,

Please recognize the many hours of blood sweat and tears _____ gave to saving others. The long years of preparation, the many hours of service, and the constant pressure of being on call took their toll on this wonderful woman. Committed to preserving and improving the quality of life for others, this doctor had an ideal bedside manner. She commiserated but never condescended, she counseled but never removed choices from her patients, and—above all—she demonstrated a reverence for life. **Come unto me all that labour and are heavy laden, and I will give you rest. Take my yoke upon you and learn of me; for I am meek and lowly in heart; and you shall find rest unto your souls. For my yoke is easy and my burden is light. St. Matthew 28**

FOR A DREAMER

Dear Lord,

Dreamers are what help us go on, they are the stuff of which a good life is made. _____ was a dreamer who helped us see important realities that we could have missed if we hadn't held our heads up high and our hearts in abeyance. He dreamed of a better world and now he has it.

FOR A DRESSMAKER

Dear Lord,

She kept us in stitches and saw your pattern in her life and ours. She kept us clothed in love and helped us pocket our secrets in ways that would hurt no one yet kept us warm. She toiled over our garments and arrayed us almost as fine as the biblical lilies of the field. She could touch material and make it go from plain to spectacular, from functional to fun. Her eyesight was failing but never her heart as she labored in light and darkness to improve the quality of our lives. She never pinned her hopes on anyone but You; please take her to your bosom and count her sins in a thimble rather than a trough. .

FOR A DRUG ADDICT OR ALCOHOLIC

Dear Lord,

How rare a person she was when she wasn't high. She was bright, cheery, loving and kind. Generous to a fault sometimes, _____ experienced the many highs and lows of life. She reached for the stars—even the ones only present in her imagination. Although her death was no doubt accelerated by her habit, she habitually showered love and consideration on us.

Come unto me all that labour and are heavy laden, and I will give you rest. Take my yoke upon you and learn of me; for I am meek and lowly in heart; and you shall find rest unto your souls. For my yoke is easy and my burden is light. (St. Matthew 28)

FOR AN EDUCATOR (SEE ALSO ACADEMICIAN, LIBRARIAN, PROFESSOR, TEACHER)

Dear Lord,

Only the blessed can teach really well and _____ _____ was blessed. As were the ones who had her as an instructor. She treated knowledge as a gift that lit the lamps of darkness and drove away demons of ignorance. She revered learning, exemplifying it in all her hobbies and habits. She inspired others to reach for the moon and stars and helped them travel faster than the speed of sound because she gave them the tools to access the secrets of the universe. Light her lamp now with your eternal oil and surround her with the greatest minds since we were never much of a challenge for her in her wisdom and wit.

FOR AN ELECTRICIAN

Dear Lord,

It feels as though the current has gone out of our life and we've lost all our juice. Our batteries are as dead as our hearts. Please restore our charge so we can continue to grow beyond this point. Take away the negatives while we enlarge upon the positives of _____'s life. He was able to correct power failures and since this feels like one of life's power failures, we'll need to transfer some of his strength and faith to our cells so we can bear this loss. He lit up our lives and we know now he'll be doing the same for You in heaven.

FOR AN EMT

Dear Lord,

It's almost ironic that one who rushed to save lives is now resting from his labors after all efforts to save his were exhausted. Please look upon your servant with kindness and compassion just as he looked on those he always helped. Emergencies were a way of life for him but we will never again be able to hear a siren without being reminded of our great loss. Help us to heal, give our hearts the oxygen they need to survive this ordeal, and fill our veins with forgetfulness for the pain and restoring powers as we mend. Keep him in your safekeeping now and forever. Amen.

FOR AN ESTRANGED FAMILY MEMBER (SEE ALSO DIVORCED/DIVORCEE)

Dear Lord,

Please let _____ know that we were here for his final moments upon the earth. We may not have always agreed with the things he did or said, or left undone, but we still loved him. Let him know that we have forgiven him just as Jesus commanded when he said, **Lord, how oft shall my brother sin against me and I forgive him? Til seven times? Jesus saith unto him, "I say not unto thee, until seven times: but until seventy times seven (to Peter) St. Matthew 21**

FOR AN EX- SPOUSE (SEE ALSO ESTRANGED, DIVORCED)

Dear Lord,

I'd like to recall the good moments because they far outnumbered the bad. _____ was one of the loves of my life; and although we split under less than ideal circumstances, it was always reassuring to know he was only a phone call away. Now, Lord, it gives me pause to wonder what I'll do without his voice, his advice, and his visions of better days. Please keep him warm and take him unto your bosom. He was a good man and deserves many rewards.

FOR A FACTORY WORKER

Life is full of toil yet _____ saw the dignity in work and worked hard to provide a good standard of living for his loved ones. He was dependable, reliable, punctual, and willing to help out anyone on the line. As he counted the days until retirement, he often did it tongue-in-cheek because he knew he was going to miss his labors and the camaraderie of his friends and co-workers. Unfortunately, it looks like we're going to miss him first.

FOR A FARMER (SEE ALSO CONSERVATIONALIST, GARDENER, ENVIRONMENTAL)

Dear Lord,

Blessed is one who toils on earth's land and makes it bear fruit. _____ was a humble, hard working servant who trusted in you and your promised harvest. He relied on the weather but also set stock in modern technology to maximize his production and minimize his risk. He lived a good life and provided for his family. He was a quiet role model and a man of his word. His wants were simple but his knowledge vast. He seemed to be comfortable in his own skin, a rare person indeed. Help him as he joins you in your eternal harvest. Amen.

AN IRISH BLESSING

May the road rise with you,
May the wind be always at your back
May the sun shine warm upon your face,
And rains fall soft upon your fields,
And until we meet again,
May God keep you in the hollow of His hand.

FOR A FATHER (SEE ALSO ADOPTED PARENT, PARENT)

Dear Lord,

Fathers are not chosen but this one easily could have been. As Mark Twain once said, "When I was a boy of fourteen, my father was so ignorant I could hardly stand to have the old man around. But when I got to be twenty-one, I was astonished at how much he had learned in just seven years". Dad, I'm sorry if I didn't always appreciate your ways and your wisdom. You were nuturing long before nuturing fathers were in vogue. You were solicitous of our happiness, proud of our achievements, and someone upon whom we could always depend. You made out of the lumber of our life not a tavern but a tabernacle, out of the words of our mouths not a reproach but a song, out of the wounds, of our heart not a permanent injury but a chance to grow. You guided us, goaded us, and carefully loved us. Oh, how you loved us! May we draw strength from that love at this time of great grief and may you go to eternity knowing the love was reciprocated a hundred fold.

FOR A FIREMAN/WOMAN

Dear Lord,

_____ has put up with enough heat his entire life. Please keep him far away from the fires of hell and purgatory. As Isaiah recognized, "He warmeth himself and said, Aha, I am warm. I have seen the fire". He was the kind of firefighter who would risk his life for another and we worried daily that he would be tested to do so. Although he was around death and its charred smell, he added a special incense to our memories and a sweet warmth to our life. He was ever faithful to the **Firefighter's Prayer**:

Lord, give me courage to face and conquer all my fears, the strength of body and spirit to help all those in need, and, Lord, protect me always. Please protect him now with as much love as he protected those whom he served for he was a good and faithful servant all the days of his life.

FOR A FISHERMAN/WOMAN

Dear Lord,

What a catch you have reeled in! You encouraged Peter and the other apostles to come and be a fisher of men but this is one fisherman who would have dropped everything if it meant going with you to collect people he loved. Although he had the patience of Job and could sit for our watching a bobbin or casting a line, he was observant and quick to cut bait when life demanded a different tact. "May the east wind never blow when he goes a-fishing" Walton, 1680. _____ would say, "...angling was an employment for his idle time which was then not idly spent...a rest to his mind, a cheerer of his spirits, a diverter of sadness, a calmer of unquiet thoughts, a moderator of passions, a procurer of contentedness; and that it begat habits of peace and patience in those that professed and practiced it." Work sometimes got in his way, and when it did he felt as though he was a salmon swimming upstream as he tried to find time for his hobby. Cut him a lot of slack now, Lord, for he never hurt anyone and the hours he spent casting about the lakes and ponds were really moments he spent pursuing you in the stream of life.

FOR A FLIGHT ATTENDANT (SEE ALSO ASTRONAUT, PILOT)

Dear Lord,

We hope your skies are friendly because you're taking on a new angel today who will make sure all the others have their seat belts fastened and are ready for take off. _____ is not afraid of heights, so we know she will be watching us from afar. Please let her maintain her pleasant ways even though you may not need coffee, juice or tea. We'd like to know some things will stay the same when we join her for all eternity. See *Celestial Pilot* at end of book.

FOR A FOOTBALL FANATIC

Dear Lord,

We know you'll look on _____'s life as a touchdown in these final hours. And although we weren't keeping score, we know that you were and You found him to be a worthy player in this game of life. He was running for daylight in his final years and constantly studied ways to improve the game. As he quarterbacked every Monday from his Lazyboy, we would hear shouts and grunts and general signs of contentment emanating from his corner in the living room. Please keep him involved in the score of his loved ones on earth as we eagerly await joining him on your field when our final two minute warning has lapsed.

FOR A FORMER LOVER

Dear Lord,

Let us remember the good times. He made me fall not only in love with him but in love with myself, thus unlocking one of life's greatest secrets—the magic of love. And when I caressed him I must admit I felt I was close to touching heaven. When I looked into his eyes I saw more than desire, I saw respect, affection, humor, and silently-pledged devotion. Although we knew such a love couldn't last, I will always treasure it as one of my finest moments. When I bought him a raincoat I stuffed the pocket with this saying "I hope you have pocketed all that I am when I am sunny. And if it rains on us, I hope you know that my love will cover you and cloak you with a thousand threads of memories and meaning". I also knew—as did he—that an affair is not always as fair as it sounds. Sometimes thorns get mixed in with the roses and what could have been a beautiful bouquet becomes instead compost with a smelly past instead of a scented future.

There have been many friends, significant others, and even paramours, but _____ was truly one of the greatest loves of my life and will never be forgotten. Although the following poem was written several years ago, (*National Anthology of College Poetry*, Dignan, 1959) perhaps it fits here:

Inevitability

Like driftwood upon the sands of Time,
My heart lay on the beach of Being
Fearful, shy, waiting for the sun—
Timid, lonely, fleeing from everyone.

You ambled by, stopping to admire
Lovingly, you caressed it;
Lifting it from the muck and mire—
Like a priest you blessed it.

You left me than—a faultless crime
For you knew such a love could never be
So like driftwood lying on the sands of Time
I wait now for the inevitable Sea.

FOR A FRIEND

From quiet homes and first beginnings,
Out to the undiscovered ends,
There's nothing worth the wear of winning,
But laughter and the love of friends.
Dedicatory Ode, Hillaire Belloc (1870-1953)

How often are we to die before we quite go off this stage? In every friend we lose a part of ourselves, and the best part. (to Swift, Dec, 5, 1732)
Alexander Pope (1688-1744)

A faithful friend is the medicine of life; A merry heart doeth good like a medicine. Love is blind; friendship just closes her eyes. Thank you for gifting me with a friend of this calibre who I know remained faithful and supportive to me 'til the end.

FOR A GAMBLER

Luck was no lady to _____ but she had fun while it lasted. The problem is it never lasted. It wasn't that she didn't love her family and friends, it's just that she was turned on by the odds and the suspense of always wondering if she'd walk away rich. She was rich in so many other ways it was sometimes hard for us to appreciate why she gambled to increase her financial status when she had all the status she ever needed with us. "Thou shalt not live within thy means Nor on plain water and raw greens. If thou must choose between the chances, choose the odd: Read the New Yorker, trust in God, and take short views". (Auden, 1979.)

The Serenity Prayer
Lord, grant me the serenity to accept the things I can not change, courage to change the things I can, and the wisdom to know the difference.

FOR A GARDENER

Dear Lord,

May we remember that to _____
__ "the poetry of earth is never dead; When all the birds are faint with the hot sun, and hide in cooling trees, a voice will run from hedge to hedge about the new mown lawn" (*On the Grasshopper and Cricket* by Keats). "In a drear-nighted December, too happy, happy tree, Thy branches ne'er remember their green felicity" (*When I Have Fears*) "Scenery is fine—but human nature is finer" (To Benjamin Bailey, 13 Mar. 1818). "Awake, O north wind; and come, thou south; blow upon my garden that the spices thereof may flow out. Let my beloved come into his garden and eat his pleasant fruits." Song of Solomon, 16. "The kiss of the sun for pardon, The song of the birds for mirth, One is nearer God's heart in a garden Than anywhere else on earth". "O, Adam was a gardener, and God who made him sees that half a proper gardener's work is done upon his knees, so when your work is finished you can wash your hands and pray for the Glory of the Garden, that it may not pass away!"

FOR A GOLFER

Dear Lord,

Even though he sometimes teed us off, for_____ no time was too early nor too late for golf. His swing, his stance, his clubs were all important to him when he approached the greens but, I think those have paled in comparison to your course, O, Lord. He will realize that everything before this time was just putting around. May he score under par as you assess his attention to the important tasks in life and may he make a hole in one when it comes to scoring with you for all eternity.

FOR A GOSSIP

Dear Lord,

How _____ loved to talk! It's too bad she won't be able to comment on this gathering today because I'm sure she would have been able to catch up on all kinds of gossip as she eavesdropped, talked, and listened to people she hasn't seen in ages. Because her gossip was never meant to be unkind but rather a way to keep up with the world, please look upon her kindly, consider her a coffee cup on wheels, and let her pass on any messages you might have in heaven.

FOR A GOVERNMENT WORKER
(SEE ALSO CITY OFFICAL)

Dear Lord,

Thankless jobs often make for thankless people but such was not the case with _____. He committed himself to the many tasks with a dedication and fealty no longer seen in today's hurry-up and wait world. He was never gruff with the people he served nor with the people who worked by his side. He was an unsung hero, quietly going about his job and doing what needed to be done on a daily basis.

FOR A GRANDCHILD (SEE ALSO ADOPTED/CHILD,INFANT/ BABY/DAUGHTER/SON)

Dear Lord,

We expected to live long enough to "see our children's children" but not to bury them, and when someone you love hurts, you hurt even more. Grant us the grace as your children to both bear this loss on our own level and to provide the support to our own children as we say goodbye to a child loved by all. We know we must accept your ways and gain wisdom in trusting that someday we'll understand the reason for such tragic pain but it's hard to see through this earthly veil with so many tears in our eyes and tears in our hearts. Hold us all to your bosom, lull us to peace with your mercy, and keep us close to each other and to your Kingdom here on earth until we are all reunited in your heaven. Amen.

FOR A GRANDFATHER (SEE ALSO FATHER/IN-LAW/FRIEND/COACH)

Dear Lord,

Gruff on the outside to others sometimes but always a marshmallow on the inside to me, Gramps, I loved you like no other giant in my life and will miss the moments I spent with you—the ones I can remember like yesterday and the ones I only heard about from you time after time after time. You helped make my childhood blessed, bountiful, happy, and safe as you modeled the life of a good man and always made time for me at your side. Although others knew you longer, no one will miss you more.

FOR A GRANDMOTHER (SEE ALSO MOTHER/IN-LAW/FRIEND)

Dear Lord,

Perhaps only grandmothers can love unconditionally but _____ made us all feel special. But let's face it—I was her favorite! At least that's how she made me feel (and if I'm being totally truthful, she made the others feel the same way in her presence). Everyone says you spoiled us grand kids; but what's to spoil? Your actions were just one of the many ways you showed us you loved us. Whether cooking our favorite meal or making a special dessert, reading us a story, or taking us for a walk, you lavished all kinds of attention on us from the day we were born. How can we be expected to forget that? And forget you? The older adults may remember you today for all kinds of reason, but I'll (we grand kids) will remember you forever for your constant good humor, your character that only we seemed to really understand, your caring from which we all benefited, and your undying support. I (we) loved you, Gramma –the same way you loved us, unconditionally, and with a passion that death can never diminish.

FOR A HANDICAPPED PERSON (SEE ALSO POEM ON SPECIAL CHILD AT THE END OF BOOK, AND EULOGY TO MY INFANT SON AT THE BEGINNING OF THIS BOOK)

Dear Lord,

Life has proved challenging for _____ since birth (his/her accident) and today, she is once again made whole. For many years and heartbreaking moments, she was made to feel less than her peers or deficient in some way. Now she's superior to all of us. Although limited in her (speech, gait, mental/physical) capacities, she was never stymied in loving us nor impacting our lives in a special way. She was more patient at times with us than we were with her, I'm afraid, and sometimes made us feel as though we were the deficient ones, the ones who didn't understand what life was all about. Her life was a hard one, but not without hope. Today may all those hopes and dreams come true as her life becomes complete and completed.

FOR A HOCKEY FAN OR PLAYER

Dear Lord,

If games are supposed to rival life, then _____ _____ scored many goals as he skated over difficulties and defended the net worth of his family and friends despite aggressive and frequent rushes. With his eye on the puck and his feet unwavering he should be able to achieve glory in a championship trophy for which earth has no match.

FOR A HOMELESS PERSON

Dear Lord,

_____ finally comes home. Himself a supplicant, he gave us comfort; himself a beggar, he distributed alms. Like the **Prodigal Son, "This my son was dead, and is alive again; he was lost, and is found". May he find all of the heavens rejoicing in his return. And may he find peace and prosperity in his eternal life for he has struggled mightily on earth and now can lay down his burdens. We will be adorned as the lilies in the valley and adored by the Shepherd always in search of his lost sheep. He has come home!**

FOR A HOUSEKEEPER

Dear Lord,

Please let her rest; she has long deserved a coffee break. _____ usually resembled the proverbial white tornado when at work and, boy, we knew enough to stay out of her way! . But we often take for granted the little things in our lives that mean so much so much of the time and only when losing them do we realize their value. Her thousands of tasks on our behalf were like that. Her attention to our home was meticulous; always shining, floors scrubbed and waxed, sheets newly changed, bathrooms scoured, clothes washed and put away, and not a speck of dust or dirt anywhere were her signature trademarks. She should have been cloned and franchised so we'd be better able to suffer the loss of one of a kind.

May _____ now be comfortable with the thought that we and she will turn to dust to await your heavenly housekeeping. And may she rest in peace from her chores and earthly toils knowing that you have a choir of angels to pick up after her. Amen.

FOR A HUNTER

You bagged a dear one, Lord.

"Under the wide and starry sky dig the grave and let me lie. Glad did I live and gladly die, and I laid me down with a will, This be the verse you grave for me: 'here he lies where he longed to be; home is the sailor home from the sea, and the hunter home from the hill'" Stevenson's *Requiem* xxi

FOR A HUSBAND

Dear Lord

Therefore shall a man leave his mother and father and shall cleave to his wife and they shall be one flesh. 24. _____ was a husband who thought matrimony a sacrament which must be treated with great reverence and respect "til death do us part". ____ _____ was truly a remarkable man, holding us up when we needed strength, holding us back when we needed restraint, and simply holding us when we need comfort or reassurance. How hard it will be, Lord, to greet the darkness without him by our side, and how difficult it will be to see the softness of the day approach away from his countenance. How alone we already feel for he knew, as did Tennyson, that "being a a husband is a full time job". Help all of us who are gathered here today to know that he and You prepared us for this over the years and that his love will still live within us--=even through our tears. He was a good man, Lord; I doubt you receive many like him at Heaven's gate. Grant him speedy entrance to your heavenly kingdom and a Lazy Boy if you could, high in the realm of your right hand where he has an unobstructed view of the game of life for those he leaves, unwillingly, behind.

FOR AN INLAW (ALL OF THESE CAN BE FOUND UNDER OTHER HEADINGS, E.G. DAUGHTER, FATHER, MOTHER, SON)

"ALTHOUGH DAUGHTER BY LAW, YOU WERE A DAUGHTER BY LOVE AND A DAUGHTER IN MY HEART", COULD BE THE PREFACE OR SOMETHING SIMILAR

DAUGHTER
FATHER
MOTHER
SON

Although we didn't spend our lives together from the instant we were born, we were family. We learned together and we grew together; and, ultimately, we laughed and loved together. I will miss you more than I could ever have imagined the first time we met. I know now: that love can come from the most unexpected places and at the most unexpected times. I hope I told him/her often enough of my deep respect and love—s/he was not just a family member at the end but a real friend who rivaled all others.

FOR AN INSURANCE AGENT

Dear Lord,

Although _____ dealt in the realities of death as an everyday occurrence, he was a man who valued life and had a zest for doing things well. He made his life's work the insurance of other's inheritances and estates. May he who looked after so many of us see dividends in Heaven's annual reports. And may he who showed so much concern for other families and the welfare of those left behind, rest knowing that the ones he left behind are not bereft and left on their own.

FOR AN INTERIOR DECORATOR

Dear Lord,

You have many mansions and it must have been time for a real overhaul in order to take _____ from our midst. From the time she was young she had a designing mind. I can't count how many times we moved the furniture or changed the colors of a room. But I can tell you that to her, interior designing was a way to bring art and aesthetics into our lives. She never tired of helping us plan, space, refurbish our surroundings to make them more functional or people-friendly. I suspect she'll even have plans for Paradise, Lord (a little to the right...no, that green clashes too much with those flowers...) so give her plenty of room and authority; even Heaven will be improved!

FOR AN INVESTMENT COUNSELOR

Dear Lord,

Show me the money....Although _____ ____ dealt in the monetary minutae of our lives, her commission was not her primary concern. Our profit and personal financial health were utmost in her mind and part of what drove her to work so hard on our behalf. Stocks and bonds, treasury notes, the Dow Jones averages, those were the tools of her trade, but a mystical language to us so she watched our daily closing and market fluctuations faithfully. Please include in her permanent portfolio special treasury notes, the kind better than gold as she joins You on the floor where she can continue to bid for us and our futures.

FOR AN IRS/TAX PERSON

Dear Lord,

Show me the money!

One could say _____ led a taxing life because no one appreciated the pressures and requirements of his job. To some extent some people even were intimidated by his presence because they didn't want him to know too much about their life styles, their spending habits, nor their extravagant hobbies. Yet he was like everyone else, a good friend, a helpful neighbor, a faithful companion, a wonderful father, and an ethical man. In your eyes, may he have already paid his estimated tax in full

FOR A JEWELER

DEAR LORD,

More precious than rubies was _____ to us. Although our eyes may not have been as trained as his, we knew a diamond when we saw one. And a diamond he was (a pearl she was). Tougher than glass but multi-faceted in his brilliance, he gave us moments and memories to treasure. His ability to shine was a given and his sense of humor insured a large collection of friends. Let his light continue to shine from afar as we mourn his loss in a world that's too often fake and too seldom a source of richness and joy.

FOR A JOGGER (SEE ALSO ATHLETE)

Dear Lord,

Although the race goes to the swift, _____ _____ ran as much for the enjoyment as for the benefits to her health. She ran to feel the wind on her face and the flowing of her blood, the liquidity of her muscles and joints and the rhythm of her movement. Whether preparing for a marathon or a short jog in the park, she always limbered up and cooled down appropriately. She knew that the human body, although a well-oiled engine, can never keep up with the mind so she made sure she didn't strain it unnecessarily. She took the same kind of pains to prepare for her final race, the one to you. May she cross the finish line a winner.

JOURNALIST/NEWSPAPER EDITOR

Dear Lord,

The printed word had such power in _____ _____'s hands yet she never abused it. She lived by words and I feel inadequate saying the things that should be said to speed her on her way. If she were writing this it would be grammatically correct and would grab you within the first five words. May my lack of skill be weighed against my storehouse of affection for her and may the words that don't see ink still find their ways to God's ear. She was a person who sought truth and never varnished it. She had integrity and an independence of thought for which some envied her but most admired her. She had the gift of gab—both in written and spoken form—and finally she had the power to weave the most incredible stories around human interest themes. She had more interest in her fellow humans than anyone else I've ever known but above all she had compassion and courage to follow a story wherever it might lead. If there is such a thing as a Pulitzer in Heaven, Lord, please make sure her name is at the top of your list of nominees.

FOR A JUDGE

Dear Lord,

_____'s whole life was about justice. He breathed it, he exemplified it, he believed in it. May he find your justice mixed with mercy for it's said that it's not justice we want when we die, it's mercy. He was a good and fair man and always sought the truth and motivation behind issues. He prided himself, justifiably, on always doing his homework so his decisions could be grounded not just in law but in life. Keep him safe and, from time to time, please try to find a few angels to call him "your honor" as Honor was his middle name.

FOR A LAWYER

Help him pass the final bar. Help us advocate his cause for a change. He spent his career serving justice, please let justice now serve him. He believed in the Professional Canon and his ethics were always above reproach. His record before the bar was sterling. In my opinion he never exulted long enough over his victories and instead lingered a long time over the cases he didn't win because those involved people and issues important to him. It's hard to believe that someone so surrounded with tomes and volumes of arcane information could keep on top of things and still maintain his sense of humor. He gave all lawyers a good name and for that we'll forgive him. He also gave money and time to charity and good causes; if for nothing else remember him for this as he enters your kingdom. Amen.

FOR A LEADER (SEE ALSO ADMINISTRATOR, BOSS, EDUCATOR)

Dear Lord,

In a world of so few leaders, _____ stood out because of his vision and vitality. He could make others see the desired end and then energize them to work toward its accomplishment. He had a passion and personal magnetism about him that attracted others to his cause. He rolled up his sleeves and shared the dignity of work. He used his mind to problem-solve and his spirit to get a following. He single-handedly brought up the bottom line then gave credit to all his co-workers and subordinates. He was a dynamo, and it's hard to believe that he is gone. There will be a real vacuum, I'm sure, while we look for someone to fill his shoes. We want to publicly thank him for being an example to us of what ordinary people can do in an extraordinary way.

FOR A LIBRARIAN (SEE ALSO EDUCATOR, TEACHER)

Dear Lord,

Shhh. Shhh. I couldn't resist saying that to her one last time because I know she would get a kick out of it. Although knowledge was her special domain, she never felt so protective of it that she would shush anyone who was earnestly in search of learning. In fact, she would engage them in a conversation so she could find out more about their search and help them successfully complete it. She encouraged little ones to read and inspired older ones to seek truth and beauty in their various forms. In many ways she was a teacher lighting the lamp and lightening our loads.

If St. Peter ever needs help with that reference Book of Life, just turn it over to her and it'll be computerized within days. Keep her mind active, God, and she'll know she's died and gone to heaven.

FOR A MAILMAN/WOMAN

Dear Lord,

Rain, snow, sleet or hail, you could always count on _____ getting through to bring us everything from junk mail to special deliveries. She knew how important it was to get mail on time and to be able to set your clock by it. Even dogs would not deter her from her appointed rounds. Her friendly smile and her recognition that special events were happening in our lives (like when she picked up our wedding and graduation invitations by the handfuls) made those moments even more special.

I guess I'm influenced heavily by early memories of a rural mail carrier when stamps were only 5 cents and my letters from college to my grandparents arrived postage due. The mailman would honk his horn as he topped the hill so they could rush out to the mailbox to bring him a nickel. I never put another stamp on my letters to them all the time I was in college after they told me that story because the ritual seemed almost as important as the writing. May the angels be honking their horns to announce the arrival of _____, a very special delivery with NO postage due.

FOR A MECHANIC

DEAR LORD,

How many times did _____ change our oil and our outlook on life? How many times did he rotate our tires, or check our batteries and our alternators? And how many times did we ask him to listen to the latest ping to tell us if we should worry? This man was more than an acquaintance and so necessary to our well being that we think there should be a special plague inscribed in the golden gates of heaven just for him saying: Top Mechanic No Longer On Duty—instead on vacation getting a lube job for all eternity. And since vehicles aren't necessary up there, perhaps he can oil the gate, keep other things in top condition, or rotate the wings on your angels every 6 million miles.

FOR A MEDICAL WORKER (SEE ALSO DOCTOR, EMT, NURSE, RADIOLOGIST)

Dear Lord,

Life was so precious to _____ that he spent most of his waking hours preserving or improving its quality for others. May he now have the same consideration as he goes in for his eternal checkup. As you check his vital signs, make sure you note how big his heart was in its capacity for loving; as you look as his brain, check out the ability to understand the pain of others and the range of compassion; and as you examine his spine, make sure you recognize that he was a stand-up guy—one we could rely on in any kind of emergency. And , finally, as you check his pulse, make sure that he knows he is only resting only until we can catch up to him. Keep him safe and in heavenly health until we meet again.

FOR A MILITARY PERSON

Dear Lord,

War is never a pleasant business but, alas, it is a necessary one and the men and women who fight for us deserve special recognition. As was said of Ulysses S. Grant and his military career. "Another name is added to the roll of those whom the world will not willingly let die...The clouds are blown away, under a serene sky he laid down his life, and the nation wept. The path to his tomb is worn by the feet of innumerable pilgrims;... even criticism hesitates lest some incautious word should mar the history of the modest, gentle, magnanimous warrior...Men without faults are apt to be men without force. A round diamond has no brilliancy. Lights and shadows, hills and valleys, give beauty to the landscape.

These heroes that shed their blood and lost their lives...

You are now lying in the soil of a friendly (grateful) country.

Therefore, rest in peace. You the mothers who sent their sons from faraway countries (or from ours) Wipe away your tears. Your sons are now lying in our bosom.

And are at peace.

After having lost their lives on this land, they have become our sons as well.

FOR A MINISTER, RABBI (SEE ALSO CLERIC, PRIEST)

Dear Lord,

How can I expect to find words to send such a worthy soul on his way?

If thou shouldst never see my face again, Pray for my soul. More things are wrought by prayer than this world dreams of. Tennyson

AN IRISH BLESSING

MAY THE ROAD RISE WITH YOU,
MAY THE WIND BE ALWAYS AT YOUR BACK
MAY THE SUN SHINE WARM UPON YOUR FACE,
AND RAINS FALL SOFT UPON YOUR FIELDS,
AND UNTIL WE MEET AGAIN,
MAY GOD KEEP YOU IN THE HOLLOW OF HIS HAND.

FOR A MODEL

Dear Lord,

Beauty was more than skin deep with _____
____ And even though Milton said beauty was nature's way to brag, she never did. She was a model in many ways; not just on the runway but in the neighborhood, in her home, and in her life. We will miss the person she was and know however fleeting her fame, her future is under contract with you for all eternity.

FOR A MOTHER (SEE ALSO, MOTHER IN-LAW, GRANDMOTHER, FRIEND, AND MY OWN MOTHER'S EULOGY IN THE INTRODUCTION OF THIS BOOK)

Mothers aren't meant to be perfect but this one very nearly was. She grew us with great care, hovered over us when we weren't looking and let us fly out of the nest—never letting us know how much her heart was hurting as she let us go. No matter how old she was, she never stopped watching her children—even when we reached middle age—for signs of improvement. An old Moorish proverb reminds us that every beetle is a gazelle in the eyes of its mother. So it was with her. And she somehow knew that children in a family are like flowers in a bouquet—always there is at least one determined to face in the opposite direction from the way the arranger desires. But this never bothered her—she encouraged us to seek our sun wherever we could find it. And if it's true that every crow thinks theirs is the blackest—we must have been obsidian in her eyes. May You, Lord, be as blind to her faults as she was to ours. And may you welcome her home.

FOR A MOVIE BUFF

_____ loved classics and knew every plot ever written. When he applied movies to real life, life sometimes came up short but it never kept him from watching for more. Soundtracks, props, background all had special meaning to him and when he gave something "2 thumbs up" you knew it surpassed even his high expectations for a great performance. We think _____ has earned a "2 thumbs up" from You, Lord. Hopefully you'll read our review before giving out your stars.

FOR A MUSICIAN

Dear Lord,

Strike up the band, a new member has just joined the great orchestra in the sky. _____ loved music almost as much as she loved life. She hummed during life's quieter moments but was never without some kind of tune brightening her day and the days of others. She was a first class (pianist, flutiest, etc.) and took great pride in her performances. We were a willing audience, feeling privileged to listen to her play. Sometimes it sounded as though instead of praying with her mouth, she was praying with her instrument. No one who loved music and made it come to life as she did could ever be anything but pure of soul. Please see that she gets to hear the angels sing, and maybe even a chance to accompany them?

FOR A NANNY

Dear Lord,

You said suffer the little children to come unto me, and ------------------------ sure suffered a lot of children in her long and distinguished career as a nanny. Many of the children she helped raise into adulthood are here today to pay her tribute and tell her, posthumously, they don't know how she managed it. She certainly didn't get them in trouble as often as they deserved and kept them out of harm's way on more than one occasion. Less than a relative but more than a best friend, Nanny, we salute you!

FOR A NEIGHBOR

Does this mean I finally get my tools/dishes back? Just joking. _____ was the best neighbor anyone could ever want. if anything, I probably still have tools/dishes of his. _____ was the kind of neighbor about whom Robert Frost wrote when he described neighbors who don't need walls between them. I will miss this guy on a daily basis. Just knocking on the door for a stick of butter or expecting him to come around with his traveling coffee cup is something I will no longer be able to take for granted. Although he wasn't Irish, this Irish blessing somehow seems appropriate: may the road rise with you, may the wind be always at your back may the sun shine warm upon your face, and rains fall soft upon your fields, and until we meet again, may God keep you in the hollow of his hand.

FOR A NEPHEW (SEE ADOPTED/ CHILD, INFANT, SON)

Dear Lord,

May _____'s parents and siblings be comforted today as we join them in our expressions of profound loss and sympathy. _____ was a child/young man who almost seemed like mine. Watching him grow develop over the years was one of life's special moments and sitting in the bleachers or behind the curtains as his many performances on life's stage took place was something we will hold forever in our hearts. Give special attention now to his parents and siblings as you call him home.

FOR A NIECE (SEE ALSO ADOPTED/ CHILD, INFANT, DAUGHTER)

Dear Lord,

May _____'s parents and siblings be comforted today as we join them in our expressions of profound loss and sympathy. _____ was a child/young girl who almost seemed like mine. Watching her grow and develop over the years was one of life's special moments and sitting in the bleachers or behind the curtains as her performances on life's stage took place was something we'll hold forever in our hearts.

FOR A NUN (SEE ALSO CLERIC, RELIGIOUS)

Sister _____ had many good habits and the greatest of these was charity. She loved people indiscriminately, without judgment and with a love as pure as the kind You fostered, O, Lord. She spent her life in service of others, never counting the cost nor demanding reimbursement for her time, her talent, her many tasks. She devoted herself to you, please insure her a special place in your heavenly home.

FOR A NURSE (SEE ALSO EMT, DOCTOR, MEDICAL WORKER)

Dear Lord,

_____ took care of the sick and infirm and made them feel well. Please do the same for her. Please reward her for all the bedpans, the IVs, the blood work, and her never ending patience. She valued her patients' dignity and gave them respect and a deep sense of comfort as she toiled to make them feel better. Hers was the reassuring voice, the soft hand, the gentle arms that helped raise them up and brought them to better health and comfort. She seemed to take St. Francis' prayer to heart (Let me seek not so much to be comforted as to comfort), please take her to heart and make her well in your eternal kingdom. Amen.

FOR AN OPTIMIST

May _____ see the cup as not just half full but finally overflowing. May she find her optimism rewarded and reinforced as she joins you for eternity. As bleak as times could become, she never despaired and as bad as we were, she never gave up on us. She was, according to Susan Morris (1947-), the embodiment of a real optimist: the human personification of spring. Help us gather strength from her habit of always seeing the positive side of everything,--even this, her death which has laid us low.

FOR A PARENT (SEE ALSO ADOPTED PARENT/GRANDFATHER/GRANDMOTHER)

All of my life I have known this wonderful person. And although I didn't always agree, like Mark Twain said, "When I was a boy of fourteen, my father was so ignorant I could hardly stand to have the old man around. But when I got to be twenty-one, I was astonished at how much he had learned in just seven years". Dad, (Mom) I'm sorry if I didn't always appreciate your ways and your wisdom. You were nuturing us long before nuturing parents were in vogue. You were solicitous of our happiness, proud of our achievements, and someone upon whom we could always depend. You made out of the lumber of our life not a tavern but a tabernacle, out of the words of our mouths not a reproach but a song, out of the wounds of our heart not a permanent injury but a chance to grow. you guided us, goaded us, and carefully loved us. Oh how you loved us! May we draw strength from that love at this time of great grief and may you go to eternity knowing the love was reciprocated a hundred fold.

Or, Mothers (fathers) aren't meant to be perfect but this one very nearly was. She grew us with great care, hovered over us when we weren't looking and let us fly out of the nest—never letting us know how much her heart was hurting as she let us go. No matter how old she was, she never stopped watching her children—even when we reached middle age—for signs of improvement. An old Moorish proverb reminds us that every beetle is a gazelle in the eyes of its mother. So it was with her. And she somehow knew that children in a family are like flowers in a bouquet—always there is at least one determined to face in the opposite direction from the way the arranger desires. But this never bothered her—she encouraged us to seek our sun wherever we could find it. And if it's true that every crow thinks theirs is the blackest—we must have been obsidian in her eyes. May You, Lord, be as blind to her faults as she was to ours. And may you welcome her home.

FOR A PESSIMIST

Dear Lord,

We think the worst that could possibly happen to _____ already has so give him a moment to gloat and say "I told you so". But we hope his dying has changed his mental attitude from finding the negatives to looking now for positives. May he find the glass not half empty but overflowing. And may his fears be extinguished now that he has faced the biggest fear of all—death—and passed through to the other side where eternal life and eternal optimism await him. Now and forever.

FOR A PHARMACIST

Dear lord,

With an apothecary of medicine, his mortar and pestle mixing compassion and a sense of humor with a storehouse of practical and professional knowledge, help _____ enter your ephemeral pharmacy. In need of no tonic, he now has everlasting waters. In need of no salve and herbs, he now has the elixir of life. May all the times he awoke in the middle of the night to help his customers, and all the hours he spent studying the latest drugs so his advice was sound be rewarded. May his concern for others and his professionalism be his attire. May his pains be attended to and any bandages or braces removed from his soul so he can join the other angels of mercy. Amen.

FOR A PHILANTROPIST

Dear lord,

I hope she left me money. Just kidding. This woman was a quiet one who did good works without a great deal of fanfare. She sought not recognition but ways to alleviate the sufferings of others (or the enhancement of the arts, etc.). She knew the value of money but also knew it had no value if not put to further your honor and glory and the worthy causes of mankind. She increased her worth by giving away her material riches and accumulating spiritual ones in their place. Although you warned us that it is easier for a camel to pass through the eye of a needle than a rich person to enter heaven, please consider her good works and her good life before she passes through your eyes for all eternity.
Charity shall cover the multitude of sins.
(1 Peter 8)

FOR A PHOTOGRAPHER

Not everything was black and white to _____ _____, but his work was often his life. And his ability to see things that most of us didn't notice was part of that gift. The lens that spoke to him often spoke to us in pictures instead of a thousand words. Because he preserved so much of the quality of the lives around him, the quality of his life was enhanced over and over again. May his portrait hang in your heavenly halls forever. Amen.

FOR A PILLAR OF THE COMMUNITY (SEE ALSO PHILANTROPIST)

May all the contributions _____ made to this community be acknowledged today and never forgotten in all the tomorrows to come.

FOR A PILOT (SEE ALSO FLIGHT ATTENDANT)

May he be flying high today as he goes beyond the blue skies to push the final envelope; and may his passing be in the accompaniment of an honor guard to recognize his good life. See also the poem entitled *Celestial Flight* at the end of this book.

FOR A PLUMBER

Although we never plumbed the depths of _____ _____, we know he was a good man and a hard worker. He was someone that could find a leak, fix it, and even clean up his mess in less than an hour. He believed in measure twice, cut once—a good philosophy for life. He knew that water seeks its own level and that people would also seek theirs. Now that he is moving up several, please help him feel that this house call is permanent and the most rewarding he's ever known. May he have sweet pipe dreams forever.

FOR A POET

May _____ find romance and wonder in this last act of yours. How did we love him? Let us count the ways. We loved in the small and great moment of the days. We loved him when night came calling our name and—whether in good mood or foul—we always loved him the same. But regardless of his words, he was a romantic at heart. May you help him find romance and beauty in the great beyond forever.. The following poem written in iambic pentameter and titled, *Ode to an Adolescent* (Dignan, 1955), could have described his adolescence and emerging adulthood.:

Reflections on Life

Life is difficult to define—it's harder still to comprehend it all.
Some days you feel simply fine; some days you wish you could end it all.
Life—uncontrolled in time—joys and heartaches are soon forgotten;
Man, the forbidden fruit desires, and at death he finds it—rotten.
"Know thyself", Socrates once said, a good and sage philosophy.
But it's easier to find faults in others than to acknowledge their presence in me.
The world in which I strive to live is a reciprocating mirror.
I get out of it what I put into it laughter, love, satisfaction, a tear.

For though I'm just a pebble on this rocky road to all eternity, (insignificant except to God—and of course to me), The lessons I have learned on the path I chose to trod Is that the trials of my life can become triumphs If I have grown in the eyes of my God.

FOR A POLICEMAN/WOMAN

Dear Lord,

This man who vowed to protect and serve is now seeking your protection for eternity. As a Police Officer _____ faithfully followed the Law Enforcement Code of Ethics because he believed that: (his) fundamental duty was to serve mankind, to safeguard lives and property, to protect the innocent against the deceptive, the weak against the oppressor or intimidator, and the peaceful against violence or disorder, and to respect the Constitutional rights of all men to liberty, equality, and justice.

He kept his private life unsullied as an example to all and maintained courage and calmness in the face of danger, scorn or ridicule. He exhibited self-restraint and was constantly mindful of the welfare of others. Honest in thought and deed both in and out of uniform, he was exemplary in obeying the laws of the land and the regulations of his department. He never acted officiously nor permitted feelings, prejudices, animosities, or friendships to influence his decisions. With no compromise for crime and relentless pursuit and prosecution of criminals, _____ wore his badge with pride and distinction, constantly striving to achieve the department's objectives and ideals in steadfast dedication to his chosen profession and a life lived serving God and his community.

FOR A PRACTICAL JOKER
(SEE ALSO CHARACTER)

Dear Lord,

This is just another one of _____'s jokes, right? He had such a great sense of humor that it's hard to grasp the finality of his passing. He made us laugh at life's jokes and could even turn a funeral into an occasion to celebrate. As we come together to bid him farewell we must grapple with the fact that this is no Houdini act—he won't be returning from back stage to cheer us up or say "I gotcha!" Please help us live with the loss of the laughter and the easy affection this man brought into our lives. Take our word for it: When it came to treating people with warmth and dignity and honoring your precepts, this man's life was no joking matter. Take good care of him and take him seriously if he tells you he's a little bored doing nothing but angelic stuff.

FOR A PRINCIPAL (SEE ACADEMICIAN, EDUCATOR, LEADER, LIBRARIAN, TEACHER)

Dear Lord,

A good principal can impact an entire community and that's just what _____ did throughout her long and distinguished career. She cared deeply about her students, her staff, her families and made academic success a reality for many kids who would never have achieved as much as they did without her high expectations and strong leadership. Remember you promised that those who take loving care of your children would be rewarded. It's only that promise that makes the loss of this great principal possible to bear. She had vision, vitality, integrity and heart. But on top of all that, she had a passion for excellence unparalleled anywhere. As she broke through one glass ceiling after another (and in such a way that she didn't have to clean up the mess), she became a pioneer and positive role model for kids of all ages.

FOR A PRISONER

Dear Lord,

Prayer Book: "Our soul is escaped even as a bird out of the snare of the fowler; the snare is broken, and we are delivered. Our help standeth in the name of the Lord who hath made heaven and earth. turn our captivity, O Lord; as the rivers in the south. They that sow in tears; shall reap in joy. He that now goeth on his way weeping and beareth forth good seed, shall doubtless come again with joy, and bring his sheaves with him...My soul fleeth unto the Lord, before the morning watch; I say, before the morning watch...The Lord looseth men out of prison; the Lord giveth sight to the blind....A joyful and pleasant thing it is to be thankful. The Lord doth build up Jerusalem and gather together the outcasts of Israel. He healeth those that are broken in heart and giveth medicine to heal their sickness. He telleth the number of the stars and calleth them all by their names. **'twas a thief said the last kind word to Christ; Christ took the kindness and forgave the theft.**

FOR A PROFESSOR (SEE ALSO ACADEMICIAN, EDUCATOR, LIBRARIAN, TEACHER)

Dear Lord,

Professor _____ lived a life of learning and was renowned not just for his own depth of knowledge and his specialty but also for his special ways with students. He inspired many young men and women to follow their dreams, chart their paths, and strengthen their basic foundations on facts—not fiction or fantasy. He emulated a mentor who found learning to be the highest calling and as he lit our lamps of knowledge, he also ignited a flame for intellectual integrity that will glow long after he is gone.

FOR A PSYCHIC

"Fear no more the heat of the sun, Nor the furious winter's rages:

Thou thy worldly task hast done, Home art gone and ta'en thy wages:

Golden lads and girls all must, As chimney-sweepers, come to dust.

Fear no more the grown o' the great, Thou art past the tyrant's stroke:

Care no more to clothe and eat; To thee the reed is as the oak:

The sceptre, learning, physic, must; All follow this, and come to dust.

Fear no more the lighting flash, Nor the all-dreaded thunder-stone;

Fear not slander, censure rash; Thou hast finish'd joy and moan:

All lovers young, all lovers must; Consign to thee, and come to dust.

No exorcisor harm thee! Nor no witchcraft charm thee!

Ghost unlaid forbear thee! Quiet consummation have: And renowned by thy grave!

Algernon Charles Swinburne (1837-1909)

FOR A RACE DRIVER/ENTHUSIAST

Dear Lord,

Speed him on his way; he is doing his final lap. Remove the checkered flags and erase his checkered past as he rounds the track this one last time. Let him hear the roar of the crowd as he roars into heaven, leaving all others behind in the smoke. And let him know he can ease up on the pedal now that he has crossed the finish line victorious and fulfilled. Amen.

FOR A RADIOLOGIST (SEE ALSO DOCTOR, EMT, MEDICAL WORKER, NURSE)

Although we always felt she could see through us, she made us want to get close and became our confidant. She was competent, caring, compassionate, and made her career a real calling. Since she helped alert others to the presence of disease and the causes of their discomfort, it shouldn't be too hard for her to feel right at home in a place where disease and discomfort are no longer present—with or without x-rays. And since you can see her heart and know the secrets invisible to the eye, let us take comfort knowing that it is only with the heart that one sees rightly and what is most important is invisible to us on earth. She already knew that. Please take advantage of her skills and give us the vision required to see beyond earth's pale as we go on without her here in our midst. Amen.

FOR A RAILROAD MAN

Pardon me lord, is that the Chattanooga Choo-Choo? Whether _____ was running the train or taking tickets from the caboose, he never deviated from the track. He was the kind of man who knew where he was headed and exactly how to get there from here. He stoked the engine of life to get maximum efficiency and speed but never put others at risk foolishly. Keep him at the throttle, dear lord, as he trains others how to live a good and meaningful life. His maxim was "If something is worth doing, it's worth doing well". He did his job faithfully & well.

FOR A REALTOR

Her plot has it all: Location, location, location. Please see she has an uninhibited view, beach access, quiet neighborhood and a large lot. She has been so meticulous in matching the right property to the right people, that her transformation to your Century Twenty One Club will be on a whole different level than the ones she's used to down here. And talk about gold jackets! These are the real thing. May she wear them well.

FOR A RELIGIOUS PERSON (SEE ALSO NUN, CLERIC, MINISTER, PRIEST RABBI)

Dear Lord,

Although _____ never consciously tried to make us feel any thing but equal to him, it was pretty hard given his goodness and obvious spirituality. He lived a life above reproach yet never reproached us for some pretty stupid and shameful acts. He loved this world but was eagerly awaiting entry into yours all the days of his life. He embraced and emulated the Beatitudes—May they bring him the promises inherent in his living them: **Blessed are the poor in spirit for theirs is the kingdom of heaven. Blessed are they that mourn for they shall be comforted. Blessed are the meek for they shall inherit the earth. Blessed are they which do hunger and thirst after righteousness for they shall be filled. Blessed are the merciful for they shall obtain mercy. Blessed are the pure in heart, for they shall see God. Blessed are the peacemakers for they shall be called the children of God.**

FOR A RESTAURATEUR (SEE ALSO COOK, CHEF)

Dear Lord,

What's on the menu? "86" is something he'll never hear again as he clears his tables and puts away the silverware of earth. He has waited on us and given us—at times—our daily bread, He has slaked our thirst and gave us an appetite for a good meal, good friends, and good living. As the Earl of Lytton said in 1861," He may live without books—what is knowledge but grieving? He may live without hope,--what is hope but deceiving? He may live without love—what is passion but pining? But where is the man that can live without dining?" He seemed to know:

Since ev'ry man who lives is born to die, And none can boast sincere felicity, With equal mind, what happens, let us bear, Nor joy nor grieve too much for things beyond our care. Like pilgrims to th' appointed place we tend; The world's an inn, and death the journey's end. 1.883 John Dryden (1631-1700)

FOR A RETIREE

Dear Lord,

"He doesn't have time for this" is what I overheard one of his fellow retirees say about _____'s funeral today. How appropriate. Retirement for _____ was a little like being a grandparent who asks why did I have to have my children first; he often asked why did I have to spend so many years working before I could sample retirement? I guess you could say as of today he is permanently retired and need no longer fear having to earn this idyllic state. He has toiled in your vineyards, he has done what you wanted of him, and he is now ready to enjoy the fruits of his labor. Welcome him and give him rest.

FOR A SAILOR (SEE ALSO BOAT ENTHUSIAST)

Dear Lord,

"Under the wide and starry sky dig the grave and let me lie. Glad did I live and gladly die, and I laid me down with a will, This be the verse you grave for me: 'here he lies where he longed to be; home is the sailor home from the sea, and the hunter home from the hill'" Stevenson's Requiem xxi

FOR A SALESPERSON

Dear Lord,

_____ was used to waiting on people and anticipating their needs and desires. Please do the same with him. If you have any bargains, please let him be the first at the booth—just don't let it be in the basement. He knew quality of fabric and lent much to the fabric of our lives; he knew a good buy and he knew a cheap sale. We will miss the integrity he had, cautioning us away from bad "bargains" and steering us to quality or something we could more easily afford. Please see that his commissions and bonuses in heaven are predicated on how well he took care of his customers on earth. And, if you get time, could you redecorate a little corner of a big cloud with a window with a view as he does his invoices and receipts. A corner office and a cloud to cushion the blow he will soon be processing as he realizes that life's final "bargain" entailed leaving us behind. We will be standing in long lines knowing that he will want to wait on us as soon as we're allowed in Your store. Keep him busy and make him happy, maybe even let him stay off his feet for longer periods of time now that he's been promoted. We always said he could sell ice to Eskimos, maybe now he can sell cotton candy and brass rings to angels.

FOR A SCIENTIST

Dear Lord,

Although _____ spent his life pursuing the scientific truths and needed proof of things in order for him to believe, he agreed with de Chardin who wrote:

Someday, after we have mastered the winds and the waves, the tides, and gravity, we will harness for God the energies of love and then, for the second time in the history of the world, man will have discovered fire.

FOR A SECRETARY (SEE CO-WORKER)

Dear Lord,

She was our type in so many ways that we hate to lose her to your labor pool this early in our association together. She might not have been able to take dictation quickly but it never stopped her from giving it. She could copy something faster than you could blink and she was wonderful at screening calls. She could work a telephone or someone else's receptionist so that our waiting time was minimal and our productivity maximal. She was cheerful, dependable, and conscientious. She kept the secret in secretary and we will miss her very much.

FOR A SPECIAL CHILD (SEE ALSO CHILD, ADOPTED, INFANT, HANDICAPPED, BABY)

"It's time again for another birth" Said the Angels to the Lord above,
"This special child will need much love". His progress may seem very slow,
Accomplishments he may not show. And he'll always require special care from the folks he meets way down there.
He may not run or laugh or play—His thoughts may seem quite far away.
In many ways he won't adapt . And he'll always be known as handicapped.
So let's be careful where he's sent. For we want his life to be content
Please, Lord, find the parents who will do this special job for You.
They will not realize right away the leading role they're asked to play
But with this child sent from above Come stronger faith and richer love.
And soon they'll know the privilege given in caring for this gift from hearven.
Their precious charge, so meek and mild,-------------
- Was heaven's very special child.

FOR A SHUT-IN

Dear lord,

Although _____ never got out that didn't stop her from being interested in the world. She was surprisingly cheerful and eager to learn about her friends and loved ones. She had a wealth of experience she loved to share and found pleasure in the smallest things, attributes that we could all benefit from. Although she never complained, I'm sure she was lonely and also at times possibly thinking: *He still loves life But O O O O how he wishes The good Lord would take him... Auden (1974)*

FOR A SINGER (SEE ALSO ACTRESS, DANCER, MUSICIAN)

So talented and so in love with life that it makes us sad to gather here today in a place in which all the music seems to have died as we mourn the death of _____. Her life seemed to have a rhythm of its own and heaven will be tempted to strike up the band since a new member has just joined the great orchestra in the sky. _____ loved music almost as much as she loved life. She hummed during life's quieter moments but was never without some kind of tune brightening her day and the days of others. She was a first class singer and took great pride in her performances. We were a willing audience, feeling privileged to listen to her sing. Sometimes it sounded as though instead of singing, she was praying for no one who loved music and made it come to life as she did could ever be anything but pure of soul. Please see that she gets to hear the angels sing, and maybe even a chance to accompany them?

FOR A SOCCER FAN OR PLAYER

What a kick _____ got out of life! And what a joy it was to watch him from the sidelines. Although he outgrew the league, he never outgrew the love for the game—the same kind of love he had for his family and friends and their little goals. As you know, he would often confront things head-on so you may have to make a few allowances for memory loss as he recounts his sins and reveals his passions. He was a good sport, a team player, and a coach to those of us who needed guidance and grit. He will be missed.

FOR A SISTER

DEAR LORD,

I take back all the mean things I said. She only deserved half of them. But she never deserved this—to die before me and so suddenly (painfully, etc). "For there is no friend like a sister in calm or story weather, to cheer one on the tedious way, To fetch if one goes astray, to lift if one totters down, To strengthen whilst one stands". 1862, *Goblin Market*—Rossetti. _____ was the kind of sister everyone wishes for but few have been granted in this lifetime. Stern when the occasion called for it, understanding when you had all but given up hope, non-judgmental about your errors but unforgiving toward those who erred against you and always there, somehow, to listen. May you grant her the ability to listen to all of us whose hearts are overflowing today with love and grief and with wordless words when saying a final farewell. Go quickly to God, my beloved sister.

FOR A SON (SEE ALSO BABY, INFANT, ADOPTED/CHILD, GRANDCHILD)

Dear Lord,

What words are there to say goodbye and god speed to a son who was the sunshine of our life? How can we possibly keep on keeping on? He reminds us of every sunrise and sunset we'll every hold dear. How can we possibly let go?

Where is that little boy I carried? Where is that little boy at play.
I don't remember growing older—when did he?
When did he get to be a beauty? When did he grow to be so tall?
Seems like only yesterday when he was small....
Sunrise, sunset, sunrise, sunset...Swiftly fly the days,
Seedlings turn overnight to sunflowers, Blossoming even as we gaze...
Sunrise, sunset, sunrise, sunset...Swiftly fly the years,
One season following another, Laden with happiness and tears....

Yes, it seemed as though "the world loved him; the women kissed his head, the men looked gravely into his wonderful eyes and children hovered and fluttered about him. I can see him now changing like the sky from sparkling laughter to darkening frowns...he knew no color-line and the Veil, though it shadowed him, and not yet darkened half his sun...Well sped, my boy, before the world had dubbed our ambition insolence, had held your ideals unattainable, and taught you to cringe and bow. Better far this nameless void that stops my life than a sea of sorrow for you." Eulogy of W.E.B.Du Bois for his son, 1899. According to Henry S. Hollland, (1847-1918), Death is nothing at all—I have only slipped away into the next room. I am I and you are you. Whatever we were to each other, that we still are. Call me by my old familiar name, speak to me in the easy way you always used. Wean no forced air of solemnity or sorrow. Laugh as we always laughed at the little jokes we enjoyed together. Play, smile, think of me; pray for me. Let my name be ever the household word that it always was. Let it be spoken without the ghost of a shadow on it. Life means all that it ever meant...There is absolute unbroken continuity. What is death but a negligible accident? Why should I be out of mind just because I am out of sight? I am waiting for you—for an interval—somewhere near just around the corner. All is well.

FOR A STAMP COLLECTOR

Dear Lord,

The hours _____ spent collecting stamps were hours spent in quiet contemplation, a state of mind suited for those who would reflect on your goodness and bounty. Whether soaking the envelopes, getting the first day issue or simply reading up on their history, _____ devoted many hours to collecting memorabilia that told him a little more each time about a favorite topic, man and his kingdom on earth. Give _____ your stamp of approval as you welcome him into your Kingdom in Heaven, now and forever. Amen.

FOR A STEP BROTHER (SEE
ADOPTED/CHILD, BROTHER,
FRIEND, GRAND/SON)

FOR A STEP DAUGHTER (SEE
ADOPTED/CHILD, FRIEND, GRAND/
DAUGHTER, SISTER)

FOR A STEP FATHER (SEE ADOPTED/
PARENT, FATHER, FRIEND,
GRANDFATHER)

FOR A STEP MOTHER (SEE
ADOPTED/PARENT, FRIEND,
MOTHER/GRANDMOTHER)

FOR A STEP SISTER (SEE ADOPTED/
CHILD, FRIEND, SISTER, GRAND/
DAUGHTER)

FOR A STEP SON (SEE
ADOPTED/CHILD, BROTHER,
FRIEND GRAND/SON)

Although we did not spend our lives together from the time we were born, we were more than just an extension of our original families. We were family in our own right and in our own way. The many adjustments that had to be made to find our place in the family pecking order taught us many skills, some positive, some not so positive, but we learned together and we grew together. And, ultimately, we laughed and loved together. I will miss _____ more than I could ever have imagined the first time I set eyes on him/her. I only wish that I knew then what I know now: That love means you never have to say you're sorry and that love can come from the most unexpected places. I hope I told _____ him/her often enough of my deep respect and admiration. Thank you for giving me not just another family member but a friend that rivaled all my friends. Amen.

FOR A STILLBORN (SEE INFANT, ADOPTED/CHILD, DAUGHTER, SON, GRANDCHILD)

Although, this baby never drew a breath outside the womb, he was living the kind of existence that perhaps resembles heaven's more than earth's. Our hearts were hurting as we left the hospital without an expected bundle of joy yet we know that he is beyond hurt and in your heavenly care. Although he was our womb-mate for only a short period of time, help him to know that his arrival was anticipated and longed for much more than his departure from our lives. And let him know, Lord, that we'll consider him our own special angel as we await the presence of others. Amen.

FOR A STUDENT (SEE ALSO DAUGHTER, SON)

Perhaps he didn't hit the books all the time but he was progressing! He used to wear a shirt that said, "College: the ten best years of my life". And now his shirts will be rainments that won't say anything they'll just speak of an eternal party, one free of assignments, tests, and early morning classes. As _____ studies his new campus, please let him know that we mourn the loss of him from our midst and that we'll try to acquire the knowledge and basic foundations of faith that will allow us to accept this abrupt and final transfer to a better place. Please grant him maximum credits, Lord.

FOR A SURGEON (SEE ALSO DOCTOR, EMT, MEDICAL WORKER, NURSE)

Dear lord,

_____ was a cut-up or at least that's what he always liked to say when being introduced for the first time to people he didn't know. But you already knew that about him, didn't you? In fact you helped guide his mind and focus his concentration as he went into the surgical theatre to do battle over bodily failures. Please reward this doctor with a dose of peace at least three times a day and please let him get out on the golf course once a week.

FOR A SWIMMER (SEE ALSO ATHLETE, JOGGER)

Dear Lord,

we're in over our heads with the loss of _____ _____ and we're drowning in our grief. Please help us lord as we try to come to grips with this great loss. Although Moses could make the Red Sea divide, we don't think we can pass through this wave of tears dividing us in two today. Please let us skip some lanes and catch up long enough to tell him goodbye and god speed.

FOR A TAILOR/SEAMSTRESS (SEE ALSO DRESSMAKER)

_____ kept us in stitches. He lined our lives with meticulous attention to detail and cared for our appearance and our general well-being. If clothes make the man, you have yourself a worthy guest to your heavenly palace and at your heavenly feast. Prepare the place you promised.

FOR A TEACHER/TELLER OF STORIES:

Eulogy for a teacher/storyteller/friend

Her life reminds me of Keebler-Ross's comments in her book on dying:

> *Think of it not as a life terminated but a life complete. Her life was complete.*

How many of us will be able to say that we have filled the spaces between the parenthesis on our tombstones with as much living as she did?

Although it was my privilege to be her boss I sometimes think she reversed the roles. She centered her life on the people she loved. Because she enjoyed teaching through storytelling, I thought I'd share a few of her favorites with you.

The first one speaks to friendship.

It's about a Little Prince who lands on earth from another planet and wants to learn the secrets of our universe. The first creature he meets is a fox whom he begs to come play with him. The fox declines saying, "I can't play with you because I'm not tamed." The Little Prince says, "What does that mean?" And the fox replies,

> *"Taming in an act too often neglected. It means to establish ties. To me you are only a little boy who is like a hundred thousand other little boys and I have no need of you. And you have no need of me. To you I am nothing more than an ordinary fox like a hundred thousand other foxes. But if you tame me,*

then we shall need each other. To me you'll be unique in all the world and to you I will be unique. If you tame me, it will be as if the sun came to shine on my life. I shall know the sound of your step, which will be different from all the others. Yours will call me, like music, out of hiding. And look, see the grain fields down yonder? I do not eat bread so wheat is of no use to me. And that is sad. But you have golden hair. Think how wonderful that will be when you have tamed me! The grain, which is also golden, will bring me back thoughts of you when you're gone. And I shall love to listen to the wind in the wheat..."

Another story _____ loved was *The Velveteen Rabbit*. It's about a stuffed animal that yearns to feel emotion. "What is real?" asks the rabbit one day. "Does it mean having things buzz inside you and a stick-out handle?"

"Real isn't how you're made said the toy horse. It's a thing that happens to you. When someone loves you for a long, long time, not just to play with but really, really loves you, then you become Real"

"Does it hurt ?"asked the Rabbit. "Sometimes" said the horse for he was always truthful, "but when you're real you don't mind being hurt".

"Does it happen all at once like being wound up or bit by bit?" asked the Rabbit

"It doesn't happen all at once" said the horse. "You become and that takes a long time. That's why it doesn't happen to people who have sharp edges. Generally by the time you are real most of your hair has been loved off and you get loose in the joints and very shabby but these things don't matter at all because once you're real, you're beautiful."

And so the Rabbit dreamed about becoming real. One day a little boy found him and took him to bed with him every night. When the boy dropped off to sleep the Rabbit would snuggle down close under his little warm chin—always with the boy's hands clasped close round him.

And so time went on and the Rabbit was very happy—so happy that he never noticed how his beautiful velveteen fur was losing its sheen and h is tale was becoming loose and all the pink rubbed off his nose where the boy had kissed him so much. so much love stirred in his little sawdust heart that it almost burst. And in his boot-button eyes that had long ago lost their polish, there came a look of wisdom and beauty.

Years passed and the Rabbit grew very old and shabby but the boy loved him just as much. He loved him so hard that he loved all his whiskers off and the pink lining to his ears turned gray and his brown spots faded. He even began to lose his shape and was so threadbare from all the hugging that he scarcely looked like a Rabbit anymore except to the boy. To him he was beautiful and that's all the Rabbit cared about because when you're real to someone you love, nothing else matters. _____ knew that when you're loved you become real and so she loved much.

She also knew that hearts were meant to wear out from use not from rust. She was a wonderful person who tamed many of us and made us real. She was wise enough to know that it's only with the heart that one sees rightly and that love lasts long after even the strongest hearts stop beating.

May this soften the pain in your hearts as we say goodbye and God Speed to a wonderful friend and teacher.

FOR A TELEPHONE/ COMMUNICATIONS SPECIALIST

dear lord,

She had our number from the first time we met. Although she could talk effectively to almost anyone, ironically, her greatest skill was an ability to listen. As you look at life's switchboard, you'd have to see her fingerprints all over the calls we made to her for comfort, for crisis, and just for company. Give her the capability to continue a line of communication with us as she goes to a greater network. Please help her keep in touch for we'll miss her far too much to let her go if we feel we'll never be able to dial her up again.

FOR A TOOL AND DIE MAKER (SEE ALSO FACTORY WORKER)

dear lord,

As _____ toiled in a hot shop with long hours and short pay, he taught us a simple lesson about life: we don't all have to be Doctors, Lawyers, and Indian Chiefs to be successful and happy; we simply have to do something we enjoy and something we're good at. He was recognized on the line as a person who would help others and one who pulled his share of the load. He was seen by his bosses as a good worker, competent and uncomplaining. May we take his lessons to heart as we wish him farewell and godspeed.

FOR A TRAVEL AGENT

_____ might say this is not the kind of trip she had in mind. We realize her travel isn't being curtailed, it's being expanded, even though that doesn't make it any easier for us, the ones she leaves behind. We won't expect her to sending us any cards this time saying "wish you were here" but it is okay if we send that message to her? We do wish she were here and know that this small planet is no longer such a fun place to be. Take good care of her until we meet again.

FOR A TRUCKDRIVER

Dear lord,

_____ loved hauling down the highway with his radio blasting and his CB at the ready. All the miles he put on his truck were mere inches compared to the mileage he put on our hearts. We still expect to see him coming around the bend or to hear his horn as he approaches the home stretch. Let him know how much we loved him, okay? 10-4, Good Buddy.

FOR AN UNCLE (SEE ALSO BROTHER)

_____ was a dearly beloved brother, husband, and father. But I want to talk today about the capacity in which I knew him best—as my uncle. Uncles can be distant and demanding, indifferent and decadent, but this uncle was loving, interested, and very much in my corner. If I was hungry, he'd sneak me a cookie when I was young, a steak as I got older; if I was thirsty, he'd give me a bottle as a baby and a bottle as a young man. If I had no place to stay he'd take me in and never lecture me. He was my friend, my confidant, my companion. I will miss him dearly.

FOR AN UNDERTAKER

I know everyone will say _____ would always let you down but they meant it as a compliment.

He would treat the dead with respect and dignity and the bereaved with compassion and concern. He would seem to understand the depths of our pain and yet he would help us make practical decisions not based on cost but on what our loved ones would want. At a time when we were extremely vulnerable, he could be trusted with our fragile lives as well as the fundamentals of the deaths of our beloved.

Now that it's his turn to be grieved over and recognized for his life's work and contributions, please give strength to his family, please give solace to his friends, and please give him a very special place in your heaven. Amen.

FOR A VETERINARIAN (SEE ALSO ANIMAL LOVER)

_____ watched over the lowly animals with care and compassion and treated them with affection at all times. When a person has that kind of consideration for beings that can't talk, it's easy to imagine the respect they give to people who can! She served us in ways to numerous to mention, always with patience and courtesy. Treat her to the best that heaven has to offer. And if you could, please slip in a pet or two, we wouldn't mind at all.

FOR A VOLUNTEER (SEE ALSO PHILANTROPIST)

dear lord,

It's a rare person who gives and doesn't count the cost. Who provides food, shelter, clothing or comfort to those in need and doesn't they are better than the less fortunate ones they serve. It's a rare person who takes the precious moments of their own lives to improve the quality of the lives of others, yet that's exactly what _____ has done for years. May she be rewarded adequately. And may you remember your promise that

Inasmuch as ye have done it unto one of the least of these my brethren, ye have done it unto me. For I was hungred and ye gave me meat; I was thirsty and ye gave me drink; I was a stranger and ye took me in; naked and ye clothed me; I was sick and ye visited me; I was in prison and you came to me.

Lord, recognize that _____ **gave her life to the unfortunate. Please take her in and shelter, feed, and clothe her in your heavenly garments now and forever. Amen.**

FOR A WAITER/WAITRESS

Dear Lord,

Perhaps she now has tips for us. But then, she always had good advice and gave it—free for the asking. She knew stories both good and bad about people; she could size you up the minute you walked in the door, she could predict the big tippers and the small spenders and yes, she could even predict what you'd order. But I don't think she predicted that she'd be leaving her station of life so soon, lord; she just wanted to sit for a minute. She was on her feet all day yet could still be cheerful. Teach us how to do that. And finally, give her the rest she deserves and the kind that was promised:

Come unto me all that labour and are heavy laden, and I will give you rest. Take my yoke upon you and learn of me; for I am meek and lowly in heart; and you shall find rest unto your souls. For my yoke is easy and my burden is light. St. Matthew 28

FOR A WELDER

Let's build a monument to a man who used blow torches like others used lighters; to a man who made light out of darkness and depth and strength out of any materials on hand. This man knew how to make sure something would adhere to a surface permanently; please help him adhere to heaven and keep us close in spirit through the molded resolve of our love.

FOR A WRESTLER (SEE ALSO ATHLETE, FAN, JOGGER)

dear lord,

What a struggle _____ had in his final moments. But what a victory is now within his grasp. Please give strength to those of us who grieve and courage to those of us whose daily lives revolved around being in his corner. He was a good and gentle man, perhaps as much bluff as bulk, as much milquetoast as muscle and as much determined as damned crazy. But we loved him. We struggle now feeling like you have us on the ropes; we won't throw in the towel but, will, instead, pick up his challenge and charge ahead with the same vigor, vitality and love of life he exhibited both in and out of the ring.

FOR A WIFE (SEE ALSO FRIEND, FORMER LOVER, HUSBAND)

Like Bridges (1844-1930) said, "Awake my heart to be loved. Awake, awake". The Bible tells us that a virtuous woman is a crown to her husband, and she was a real treasure!" This is now bone of my bones, and flesh of my flesh; she shall be called woman because she was taken out of man. 23 Old Testament

Abide with me; fast falls the eventide;
The darkness deepens; Lord, with me abide;
When other helpers fail, and comforts flee,
Help of the helpless, O, abide with me
Swift to its close ebbs out life's little day;
Earth's joys grow dim, its glories pass away;
Change and decay is all around I see;
O, Thou, who changest not, abide with me.
H.F. Lyte (1793-1847)

Doubt thou the stars are fire;
Doubt that the sun doth move;
Doubt truth to be a liar;
But never doubt I love(d).

My dear wife,

No one knew me as you did. No one loved me as you did. No one cared for all my worldly and spiritual needs as you did. Although I never told you enough how much I loved you and others may not have guessed at the depth of my affection for you, you did. Although I was never as patient nor as kind and tolerant of other people and never practiced the many niceties that should go on among people, I was forgiven because you did. How will I get by without you? How will I face each morning and welcome each night without you? Please give me the strength to move on from this abyss of grief and carry you with me throughout the days and nights that are given to me for the rest of my life. And let me remember the good times we had together for *Time Remembered is Grief Forgotten*.

"For winter's rains and ruins are over, And all the season of snows and sins; The days dividing lover and lover, The light that loses, the night that wins; And time remembered is grief forgotten, And frosts are slain and flowers begotten, And in green underwood and cover Blossom by blossom the spring begins...Before the beginning of years There dame to the making of man Time with a gift of tears, Grief with a glass that ran... Strength without hands to smite, Love that endures for a breath; Night, the shadow of light, And Life, the shadow of death....From too much love of living, From hope and fear set free, We thank with brief thanksgiving Whatever gods may be..." (John Donne). Rest in peace, Remembered One.

EULOGIES FOR UNIQUE CIRCUMSTANCES

FOR ONE WHO DIED OF AIDS

Dear Lord,

As we gather today to say farewell and god speed to _____, let us recognize his courage and his deep devotion to those he loved. Let us acknowledge that he chose a difficult path and he was truthful about his choices, accepting of the consequences, and proud that he stayed the course. We believe that he will be judged not by us but by the lord that made him, the lord that promised him a heavenly reward if he believed in him. He was faithful 'til the end.

St. Luke: (7:47) Her sins which are many are forgiven for she has loved much.

If ye have faith as a grain of mustard seed, ye shall say unto this mountain, Remove hence to yonder place; and it shall remove. St. Matthew 17:20

FOR ONE WHO DIED
OF AN ACCIDENT

Dear Lord,

Our hearts are torn asunder. Not only did we love _____ but we didn't even get time to say goodbye. Tell her all the things we should have told her before she left home that day and keep repeating them to ease our minds. Peace will come to us late we know but we ask you to help us accept the things we can not change, grant us courage to change the things we can, and the wisdom to know the difference.'

FOR ONE WITH ALZHIEMERS

"He died in a good old age, full of days, riches, and honour" 1 Chronicles "for what is life? It is even a vapour, that appearth for a little time, and then vanisheth away" James 4:14 "Be thou faithful unto death, and I will give thee a crown of life". Revelation 10; "I will not blot out his name out of the book of life" 3:5

FOR ONE BEDRIDDEN

Isaiah: But they that wait upon the Lord shall renew their strength; they shall mount up with wings as eagles, they shall run, and not be weary; and they shall walk and not faint. _____ has spent so much time in bed, give her the grand tour and a walk in Paradise, O, Lord.

FOR ONE WHO DIED OF ASPHYXIATION/FIRE

Dear lord,

As _____ took his last breath, he called your name. And you gave him courage to face and conquer his fears, the strength to still think of those in need and the breeze of your cooling spirit. And the fire became not a fire, but a simple fever—one that whispered I love you.

May he support us all the day long, till the shades lengthen and the evening comes and the busy world is hushed, and the fever of life is over, and our work is done. Then in his mercy may he give us a safe lodging, and a holy rest, and peace at last. (Cardinal Newman)

FOR ONE WHO DIED OF CANCER

Dear Lord,

The pain of watching someone you love die slowly is a sort of death by itself. _____ wasn't afraid of dying; she said she was simply afraid that the pain would be too great before she was called home to you. Thank you for easing her pain in her last moments and for giving us time to say goodbye while she was still alive to hear it.

FOR ONE WHO DIED OF PNEUMONIA

Dear Lord,

_____'s death was so unlike his life. His every breath was a testimony to you and a declaration of love to us. Help us to accept that he breathes no more.

FOR ONE WHO DIED OF SUCIDE

"All this buttoning and unbuttoning" 18th century suicide note. "It matters not how a man dies but how he lives. The act of dying is not of importance, it lasts so short a time". Johnson, 10/26/1769   "Love is as strong as death" Isaiah, 8:6

Michael Henchard's Will: That Elizabeth-Jane Farfrae be not told of my death, or made to grieve on account of me & that I not be buried in consecrated ground & that no sexton be asked to toll the bell & that nobody is wished to see my dead body & that no murners walk behind me at my funeral & that no flours be planted on my grave & that no man remember me. To this I put my name. (Hardy, Ch. 45 The Mayor of Casterbridge (1894) "I am gone into the fields to take what this sweet hour yields; Reflection, you may come tomorrow, sit by the fireside with Sorrow. You with the unpaid bill, Despair, you, tiresome verse-reciter Care, I will pay you in the grave Death will listen to your stave. (To Jane: The Invitation, Shelley (1792-1822)

Perhaps _____ felt like the author Frank O'Malley in 1930 who said, **Life is just one damned thing after another. Or Browning's Paracelsus (1806-61) when he said, I give up the fight; let there be an end, A privacy, an obscure nook for me. I want to be forgotten even by God.**

FOR ONE WHO DIED SUDDENLY

Wilt thou forgive that sin, where I begun, which is my sin, though it were done before? Wilt thou forgive those sins through which I run and do them still, though still I do deplore? When thou hast done, thou hast not done, for I have more. Will thou forgive that sin, by which I' have won others to sin, and made my sin their door? Wilt thou forgive that sin which I did shun A year or two, but wallowed in a score? When thou hast done, thous hast not done. For I have more....John Donne

Dear Lord,

We recognize that _____'s death was sudden; in most ways that made it easier for her but harder for us since we didn't get to say goodbye. If she had any unfinished business, may the prayer above take care of her omissions or commissions and help her find her way into heaven as quickly as she left this earth. Tell her we love her and will keep her memory alive as long as we can think and speak. Help us with our grief which seems too great to bear.

FOR ONE WHO DIED WITH HEART PROBLEMS

"If I have faltered more or less
In my great task of happiness;
If I have moved among my race
And shown no glorious morning face;
If beams from happy human eyes
Have moved me not; if morning skies,
Books, and my food, and summer rain
Knocked on my sullen heart in vain—
Lord, thy most pointed pleasure take
And stab my spirit wide asweake;
Or Lord, if too obdurate I,
Choose thou, before that spirit die,
A piercing pain, a killing sin,
And to my dead heart run them in! (Stevenson, *The Celestial Surgeon* xxii, 1850-1894)

FOR ONE WHO DROWNED
(SEE ALSO SWIMMER)

Dear Lord,

They claim that drowning is the softest way to die. That there is a kind of euphoria at the last minute that gives the dying peace before unconsciousness sets in. We can take some comfort in that fact if it's true; however, in the final analysis, "It matters not how a man dies, but how he lives. The act of dying is not of importance, it lasts so short a time. Johnson, Oct. 26, 1769. _____ lived a good and full life. Thank you for blessing us with her as long as you did. Elstow said, "With thanks to God we know the way to heaven, to be as ready by water as by land, and therefore we care not which way we go." When threatened with drowning by Henry VIII., 1615

FOR ONE WHO SUFFERED

Dear Lord,

Perhaps it could be said of
_____ He still loves life. but O O O O how he wishes the good Lord would take him.. Auden (1974) **Come unto me all that labour and are heavy laden, and I will give you rest. Take my yoke upon you and learn of me; for I am meek and lowly in heart; and you shall find rest unto your souls. For my yoke is easy and my burden is light. St. Matthew 28**

FOR A VICTIM OF ABUSE

Dear Lord,

Jesus said, "Whosoever shall receive one such little child in my name receiveth me. But whoso shall offend one of these little ones which believe in me, it were better for him that a millstone were hanged about his neck, and that he were drowned in the depth of the sea." (St. Matthew, 5) Help us with our grief and help us seek justice not revenge and

Where there is now hatred, let me sow love.....
Where there is injury, pardon,
Where there is doubt, faith,
Where there is despair, hope,
Where there is darkness, light,
And where there is sorrow, joy.
O, Divine Master, grant that I may not so much seek
To be consoled, as to console,
To be understood as to understand;
To be loved as to love;
For it is in giving that we receive—
It is in pardoning that we are pardoned
And it is in dying that we are born to eternal life.
Let me seek not so much to be understood
As to understand.........the reasons for this loss and the impact on my life forever after. Amen.

FOR A VICTIM OF DRUNK DRIVING (SEE ALSO VICTIM OF AN ACCIDENT)

Dear Lord,

As we mourn the loss of innocent life, let us put aside the hatred and anger we feel over the driver who was drunk. Let us seek justice, not revenge. Let us follow the words of St. Francis

Help us with our grief and help us seek justice not revenge.
Where there is now hatred, let me sow love.....
Where there is injury, pardon,
Where there is doubt, faith,
Where there is despair, hope,
Where there is darkness, light,
And where there is sorrow, joy.
O, Divine Master, grant that I may not so much seek
To be consoled, as to console,
To be understood as to understand;
To be loved as to love;
For it is in giving that we receive—
It is in pardoning that we are pardoned
And it is in dying that we are born to eternal life.
Let me seek not so much to be understood
As to understand....the reasons for this loss and the impact of my life forever after. Amen..

FOR A VICTIM OF HOMICIDE

Dear Lord,

Not only was _____ murdered but so was part of my soul. Please help me become whole again so I can be strong for the rest of the family and keep his memory alive for love is as strong as death (Isaiah 8:6)

FOR A VICTIM OF HIT AND RUN (SEE ALSO ACCIDENT, DRUNK DRIVING, HOMICIDE)

Dear Lord,

At least he never knew what hit him.
Prayer for the Dead

Let us pray for all the faithful departed; o God, Creator and Redeemer of all men, we beseech Thee to grant to the Soul of thy servant the remission of his/her sins so that by our prayers she/he may obtain the indulgence for which they long. O lord who reigns and lives world without end.

V. Eternal rest give unto them O Lord

R. And let perpetual light shine upon them. May they rest in peace. Amen.

FOR A VICTIM OF RAPE

Dear Lord,

When one's body is so assaulted, it's hard for us to let go of the violent images. Please grant her peace and us some sort of rest from the nightmares

Psalm 26: The lord is my light and my salvation; whom should I fear? The Lord is my life's refuge; of whom should I be afraid: When evildoers come at me to devour my flesh, my foes and my enemies themselves stumble and fall. Though an army encamp against me, my heart will not fear; though war be waged upon me, even then will I trust. (Only) One thing I ask of the Lord; this I seek: to dwell in the house of the Lord all the days of my life, that I may gaze on the loveliness of the Lord and contemplate his temple. For he will hide me in his abode in the day of trouble; he will conceal me in the shelter of his tent, he will set me high upon a rock. Even now my head is held high above my enemies to every side. And I will offer in his tent sacrifices with shouts of gladness; I will sing and chant praise to the Lord.

Time Remembered is Grief Forgotten

For winter's rains and ruins are over, And all the season of snows and sins; The days dividing lover and lover, The light that loses, the night that wins; And time remembered is grief forgotten, And frosts are slain and flowers begotten, And in green underwood and cover Blossom by blossom the spring begins...Before the beginning of years There came to the making of man Time with a gift of tears, Grief with a glass that ran... Strength without hands to smite, Love that endures for a breath; Night, the shadow of light, And Life, the shadow of death....From too much love of living, From hope and fear set free, We thank with brief thanksgiving Whatever gods may be That no man lives forever, That dead men rise up never; That even the weariest river Winds somewhere safe to sea."

FOR A VICTIM OF BURGLARY/ROBBERY

DEAR LORD,

Remember your promise to keep us from the thieves in the night. We know we will never know the appointed hour of our own deaths but help us accept that it was _____'s time to die and that we should see this not as a life terminated but a life complete.

Psalm 26: The lord is my light and my salvation; whom should I fear? The Lord is my life's refuge; of whom should I be afraid: When evildoers come at me to devour my flesh, my foes and my enemies themselves stumble and fall. Though an army encamp against me, my heart will not fear; though war be waged upon me, even then will I trust. (Only) One thing I ask of the Lord; this I seek: to dwell in the house of the Lord all the days of my life, that I may gaze on the loveliness of the Lord and contemplate his temple. For he will hide me in his abode in the day of trouble; he will conceal me in the shelter of his tent, he will set me high upon a rock. Even now my head is held high above my enemies on every side. And I will offer in his tent sacrifices with shouts of gladness; I will sing and chant praise to the Lord.

EXCERPTS FROM THE BIBLE AND OTHER FAMOUS SOURCES

Psalm 17: The breakers of death surged round about me, the destroying floods overwhelmed me; the cords of the nether world enmeshed me, the snares of death overtook me. In my distress, I called upon the Lord and cried out to my God; from his temple he heard by voice, and my cry to him reached his ears.

The earth swayed and quaked; the foundations of the mountains trembled and shook when his wrath flared up. Smoke rose from his nostrils and a devouring fire from his mouth that kindled coals into flame. And he inclined the heavens and came down with dark clouds under his feet. He mounted a cherub and flew, borne on the wings of the wind. And he made darkness the cloak about him; dark, misty rain-clouds his wrap. From the brightness of his presence coals were kindled to flame. And the Lord thundered from Heaven; the Most High gave forth his voice; he sent forth his arrows to put them to flight with frequent lightnings he routed them. Then the bed of the sea appeared, and the foundations of the world were laid bare, at the rebuke of the Lord, at the blast of the wind of his wrath. He reached out from on high and grasped me; he drew me out of the deep waters. He rescued me from my might enemy and from my foes, who were too powerful for me. They attacked me in the day of my calamity but the

Lord came to my support. He set me free in the open, and rescued me, because he loves me.

Turn, Turn, Turn (or to every thing there is a season) To every thing there is a season, and a time to every purpose under heaven;

A time to be born and a time to die; a time to plant, and a time to pluck up that which is planted; a time to kill and a time to heal; a time to break down and a time to build up; a time to weep, and a time to laugh; a time to mourn and a time to dance; a time to cast away stones and a time to gather stones together; a time to embrace and a time to refrain from embracing; a time to get and a time to lose; a time to keep and a time to cast away; a time to rend and a time to sew; a time to keep silence and a time to speak; a time to love, and a time to hate; a time of war and a time of peace. Ecclesiastes (3:1)

Come unto me all that labour and are heavy laden, and I will give you rest. Take my yoke upon you and learn of me; for I am meek and lowly in heart; and you shall find rest unto your souls. For my yoke is easy and my burden is light. St. Matthew 28

AN IRISH BLESSING

MAY THE ROAD RISE WITH YOU, MAY THE WIND BE ALWAYS AT YOUR BACKMAY THE SUN SHINE WARM UPON YOUR FACE, AND RAINS FALL SOFT UPON YOUR FIELDS, AND UNTIL WE MEET AGAIN, MAY GOD KEEP YOU IN THE HOLLOW OF HIS HAND.

THE SERENITY PRAYER

Lord, grant me the serenity to accept the things I can not change, courage to change the things I can, and the wisdom to know the difference.

PRAYER OF ST. FRANCIS OF ASSISSI

Lord, make me an instrument of your peace,
where there is hatred, let me sow love,
Where there is injury, pardon,
Where there is doubt, faith,
Where there is despair, hope,
Where there is darkness, light,
And where there is sorrow, joy.
O, Divine Master, grant that I may not so much seek
To be consoled, as to console,
To be understood as to understand;
To be loved as to love;
For it is in giving that we receive---
It is in pardoning that we are pardoned
And it is in dying that we are born to eternal life.

THE MEMORARE

Remember, O most gracious Virgin Mary, that never was it known that any one who fled to thy protection, implored thy help, and sought thy intercession was left unaided. Inspired with this confidence, I fly unto thee, O Virgin of Virgins, my Mother to thee I come, before thee I stand sinful and sorrowful. O Mother of the Word Incarnate! Despise not my petions, but, in thy mercy, hear and answer me Amen.

Our Father
Our Father, who art in Heaven, hallowed by thy name. Thy kingdom come, thy will be done on earth as it is in heaven, Give us this day our daily bread and forgive us our trespasses as we forgive those who trespass against us. And lead us not into temptation for thine is the kingdom and the power and the glory forever. Amen

Hail Mary
Hail Mary, full of grace. The lord is with thee. Blessed art thou among women and blessed is the fruit of the womb, Jesus. Holy Mary, Mother of God pray for us now and at the hour of our death. Amen.

The Beatitudes
Blessed are the poor in spirit for theirs is the kingdom of heaven. Blessed are they that mourn for they shall be comforted. Blessed are the meek for they shall inherit the earth. Blessed are they which do hunger and thirst after righteousness for they

shall be filled. Blessed are the merciful for they shall obtain mercy. Blessed are the pure in heart, for they shall see God. Blessed are the peacemakers for they shall be called the children of God.

PSALM 23

The Lord is my Shepherd. I shall not want. He maketh me to lie in green pastures and lead me forth beside the waters of comfort. Yea, though I walk through the valley of the shadow of death, I will fear no evil; for thou art with me; thy rod and thy staff shall comfort me. Thou shalt prepare a table before me against them that trouble me; thou has anointed my head with oil, and my cup shall be full. But thy loving-kindness and mercy shall follow me all the days of my life: and I will dwell in the house of the Lord for ever.

PRAYER FOR THE DEAD

Let us pray for all the faithful departed; o God, Creator and Redeemer of all men, we beseech Thee to grant to the Soul of thy servant the remission of his/her sins so that by our prayer she/he may obtain the indulgence for which they long. O lord who reigns and lives world without end. Amen.

V. Eternal rest give unto them O Lord

R. And let perpetual light shine upon them. May they rest in peace. Amen.

Consider the lilies of the field, how they grow; they toil not, neither do they spin; and yet I say to you that even Solomon in all his glory was not arrayed like one of these. St. Matthew, 28

Isaiah: But they that wait upon the Lord shall renew their strength; they shall mount up with wings as eagles, they shall run, and not be weary; and they shall walk and not faint.

The last enemy that shall be destroyed is death. 1 Corinthians 6

Love is as strong as death Isaiah 8:6

- death where is thy sting, o Grave, where is thy victory? Ephesians 55
- Corinthians 3"5 Our sufficiency is of God who also has made us able ministers of the new Testament; not of the letter but of the spirit; for the letter killeth but the spirit giveth life

We have this treasure in earthen vessels 4:7 We know that if our earthly tabernacle of this house were dissolved, we have a building of God, a house not made of hands, eternal in the heavens 5:1

St. Luke: (7:47) Her sins which are many are forgiven for she has loved much.

If ye have faith as a grain of mustard seed, ye shall say unto this mountain, Remove hence to yonder place; and it shall remove. (St. Matthew 17:20)

Wilt thou forgive that sin, where I begun, which is my sin, though it were done before? Wilt thou forgive those sins through which I run and do them still, though still I do deplore? When thou hast done, thou hast not done, for I have more. Will thou forgive that sin, by which I have won others to sin, and made my sin their door? Wilt thou forgive that sin which I did shun a year or two, but wallowed in a score? When thou hast done, thou hast not done. For I have more (Hymn to God the Father)

Inasmuch as ye have done it unto one of the least of these my brethren, ye have done it unto me. For I was hungered and ye gave me meat; I was thirsty and ye gave me drink; I was a stranger and ye took me in; naked and ye clothed me; I was sick and ye visited me; I was in prison and you came to me.

Behold, I shew you a mystery: We shall not all sleep, but we shall be changed, In a moment, in the twinkling of an eye, at the last trump; for the trumpet shall sound, and the dead shall be raised incorruptible, and we shall be changed. For this corruptible must put on incorruption, and this mortal must put on immortality. (2 Corinthians 51)

Proverbs: Even in laughter, the heart is sorrowful 14:13

He will swallow up death in victory; and the Lord God will wipe away tears from all faces. Isaiah, 8

But they that wait upon the Lord shall renew their strength; they shall mount up with wings as eagles; they shall run, and not be weary; and they shall walk, and not faint. Isaiah, 31

Go thy way, eat thy bread with joy, and drink thy wine with a merry heart; for God now accepteth thy works. Ecclesiastes 7

The Lord is my Sherherd; therefore can I lack nothing. He shall feed me in a green pasture; and lead me forth beside the waters of comfort. Yea, though I walk through the valley of the shadow of death, I will fear no evil: for thou art with me; thy rod and thy staff comfort me. Thou shalt prepare a table before me against them that trouble me; thou hast anointed my hear with oil, and my cup shall be full. But thy loving kindness and mercy shall follow me all the days of my life; and I will dwell in the house of the Lord forever. Psalm 23.

EXCERPTS FROM THE *PRAYER BOOK*

I will life mine eyes unto the hills: from whence cometh my help. My help cometh even from the Lord; who hath made heaven and earth. He will not suffer thy foot to be moved; and he that keepth thee will not sleep. Behold he that keepeth Israel: shall neither slumber nor sleep. The Lord himself is thy keeper: the Lord is thy defence upon the right hand; so that the sun shall not burn thee by day; neither the moon by night. 121:1

My soul fleeth unto the Lord: before the morning watch, I say, before the morning watch. 6

O, Lord, thou hast searched me out, and known me: thou knowest my down-sitting, and mine uprising; thou understandest my thoughts long before... Such knowledge is too wonderful and excellent for me; I cannot attain unto it. Whither shall I go then from thy Spirit: or whither shall I go then from thy presence? If I climb up into the heaven, thou art there: if I go down to hell, thou are there also. If I take the wings of the morning: and remain in the uttermost parts of the sea; even there also shall thy hand lead me; and thy right hand shall hold me. If I say Peradventure, the darkness shall cover me: then shall my night be turned to day. Yea the darkness is no darkness with thee, but the night is as clear as the day: the darkness and light to thee are both alike.

Where your treasure is, there will your heart be also. (St. Matthew, 21)

I do not set my life at a pin's fee; And for my soul, what can it do to that, Being a thing immortal as itself?

Doubt thou the stars are fire;
Doubt that the sun doth move;
Doubt truth to be a liar;
But never doubt I love(d).

To be or not to be: that is the question: Whether 'tis nobler in the mind to suffer the slings and arrows of outrageous fortune, or to take arms against a sea of troubles, and by opposing end them: To die: to sleep; No more; and, by a sleep to say we end the heart-ache and the thousand natural shocks that flesh is heir to is a consummation devoutly to be wish'd . to did, to sleep to sleep perchance to dream; aye, there's the rub for in that sleep of death what dreams may come when we have shuffled off this mortal coil must give us pause.

ABSENCE is to love what wind is to fire; it extinguishes the small, it enkindles the great. Comte De Bussy-Rabutin, (1618-1693)

All this buttoning and unbuttoning -------*18th century suicide note*

Pur down upon us the abundance of mercy; forgiving us those things hereof our conscience is afraid. 12th Sunday after Trinity (English Prayerbook)

It matters not how a man dies, but how he lives. The act of dying is not of importance, it lasts so short a time. Johnson, Oct. 26, 1769

About Pompey the Great (1910), John Masefield wrote, Death opens unknown doors. It is most grand to die.

Call no man happy till he dies, he is at best but fortunate. Herodotus, Histories, i.32

A SPECIAL CHILD

"It's time again for another birth"
Said the Angels to the Lord above,
"This special child will need much love,"
His progress may seem very slow
Accomplishments he may not show.
And he'll always require special care
From the folks he meets way down there.
He may not run or laugh or play
His thoughts may seem quite far away
In many ways he won't adapt
And he'll always be known as handicapped.
So let's be careful where he's sent
For we want his life to be content
Please, Lord, find the parents who
Will do this special job for You.
They will not realize right away
The leading role they're asked to play
But with this child sent from above
Come stronger faith and richer love.
And soon they'll know the privilege given
In caring for this gift from hearven.
Their precious charge, so meek and mild,------------
---,
Was heaven's very special child

TIME REMEMBERED IS GRIEF FORGOTTEN

For winter's rains and ruins are over, And all the season of snows and sins; The days dividing lover and lover, The light that loses, the night that wins; And time remembered is grief forgotten, And frosts are slain and flowers begotten, And in green underwood and cover Blossom by blossom the spring begins...Before the beginning of years There came to the making of man Time with a gift of tears, Grief with a glass that ran... Strength without hands to smite, Love that endures for a breath; Night, the shadow of light, And Life, the shadow of death....From too much love of living, From hope and fear set free, We thank with brief thanksgiving Whatever gods may be That no man lives forever, That dead men rise up never; That even the weariest river Winds somewhere safe to sea."

Death be not proud, though some have called thee mighty and dreadful, for thou art not so, for those whom thou think'st thou dost overthrow die not, poor death, not yet canst thou kill me. From rest and sleep, which but thy pictures be, much pleasue, then from thee much more must flow, and soonest our best men with thee doth go, rest of their bones and soul's delivery.   John   Donne (1571-1631)

Heart speaks to heart (motto for cardinal's coat of arms 1879)

There are so few can grow old with grace. No. 263 Sir Richard Steele (1672-1729)

What, after all, is a halo? It's only one more thing to keep clean.

There is no greater sorrow than to recall a time of happiness in misery. Dante 1265-1321)

Not in Utopia—subterranean fields—or some secreted island, heaven knows where! But in this very world, which is the world of all of us,--the place where, in the end we find our happiness, or not at all!

IF BY RUDYARD KIPLING

If you can keep your head when all about you
Are losing theirs and blaming it on you,
If you can trust yourself when all men doubt you,
But make allowance for their doubting too;
If you can wait and not be tired by waiting,
Or being lied about, don't deal in lies,
Or being hated, don't give way to hating
And yet don't look too good, nor talk too wise:
If you can dream and not make dreams your master;
If you can think—and not make thoughts your aim;
If you can meet with Triumph and Disaster
And treat those two impostors just the same.
If you can make one heap of all your winnings
And risk it on one turn of pitch and toss,
And lose, and start again at your beginnings
And never breathe a word about your loss.
If you can talk with crowds and keep your virtue,
Or walk with Kings—nor lose the common touch,
If neither foes nor loving friends can hurt you,
If all men count with you, but none too much;
If you can fill the unforgiving minute
With sixty seconds' worth of distance run,
Yours is the Earth and everything that's in it,
And—which is more—you'll be a Man, my son!

REJOICE BY BRIDGES (1844-1930)

"Rejoice ye dead, where'er your spirits dwell,
Rejoice that yet on earth your fame is bright,
And that your names, remembered day and night,
Live on the lips of those who love you well.

DESIDERADA

Go placidly amid the noise and haste, and remember what peace there may be in silence. As far a possible, without surrender, be on good terms with all persons. Speak your truth quietly and clearly; and listen to others, even the dull and ignorant; they too have their story.

Avoid loud and aggressive persons; they are vexations to the spirit. If you compare yourself with others, you may become vain and bitter; for always there will be greater and lesser persons than yourself. Enjoy your achievements as well as your plans.

Keep interested in your own career, however humble; it is a real possession in the changing fortunes of time. Exercise caution in your business affairs; for the world is full of trickery. But let this not blind you to what virtue there is; many persons strive for high ideals; and everywhere life is full of heroism.

Be yourself. Especially, do not feign affection. Neither be cynical about love; for in the face of all aridity and disenchantment it is perennial as the grass. Take kindly the council of the years, gracefully surrendering the things of youth. Nurture strength of spirit to shield you in sudden misfortune. But do not distress yourself with imaginings. Many fears are born of fatigue and loneliness. Beyond a wholesale discipline, be gentle with yourself.

You are a child of the universe, no less than the trees and the stars; you have a right to be here. And whether or not it is clear to you, no doubt the universe is unfolding as it should.

Therefore be at peace with God, whatever you conceive Him to be, and whatever your labors and aspirations, in the noisy confusion of life keep peace with your soul.

With all its sham, drudgery and broken dreams, it is still a beautiful world. Be careful. **Strive to be happy.** God defend me ...for the joy of love is too short, and the sorrow thereof, and what cometh thereof, dureth over long." (Sir Thomas Malory d. 1471)

No, the heart that has truly lov'd never forgets, But as truly loves on to the close, As the sun-flower turns on her god, when he sets, the same look which she she turn'd when he rose. Thomas Moore (1779-1852)

If thou shouldst never see my face again, Pray for my soul. More things are wrought by prayer than this world dreams of. Tennyson

In the depths of winter I finally learned that there was in me an invincible summer.

"Wise Wretch! With pleasures too refin'd to please,
With too much spirit to be e'er at ease,
With too much quickness e'er to be taught,
With too much thinking to have common thought,
You purchase pain with all that joy can give,
And die of nothing but a rage to live.
Alexander Pope, 1688-1744

The joys of marriage are the heaven on earth,
Life's paradise, great princess, the soul's quiet,
Sinews of concord, earthly immortality,
Eternity of pleasures, no restoratives
Like to a constant woman.
John Ford 1863-1639

To cure the mind's wrong bias, spleen,
Some recommend the bowling green,
Some hilly walks; all, exercise,
Fling but a stone, the giant dies.
Laugh and be well.   Matthew
Green, 1696-1737

Out-worn heart, in a time out-worn,
Come clear of the nets of wrong and right;
Laugh heart, again, in the grey twilight,
Sigh, heart again, in the dew of the morn.
Yeats (1865-1939)

There are only two lasting bequests we can hope to give our children. One of these is roots; the other is wings.
Hodding Carter

To live in hearts we leave behind is not to die.
T. Campbell
Abide with me; fast falls the eventide;
The darkness deepens; Lord, with me abide;
When other helpers fail, and comforts flee,
Help of the helpless, O, abide with me

Swift to its close ebbs out life's little day;
Earth's joys grow dim, its glories pass away;
Change and decay is all around I see;
O, Thou, who changest not, abide with me.
H.F. Lyte (1793-1847)

On Aging: In a dream you are never eighty.
Anne Sexton (1928-1974)

This above all: To Thine own self be true, And it must follow, as the night the day, Thou canst not then be false to any man.   Shakespeare

Here lies a poor woman who always was tired,
For she lived in a place where help wasn't hired.
Her last words on earth were, Dear friends I am going
Where washing ain't done nor sweeping nor sewing,
And everything there is exact to my wishes,
For there they don't eat and there's no washing of dishes...
Don't mourn of me now, don't mourn for me never,
For I'm going to do nothing for ever and ever. Epitaph in Bushey Churchyard, 1860

I expect to pass through this world but once; any good thing therefore that I can do, or any kindness that I can show to any fellow-creature, let me do it now; let me not defer or neglect it, for I shall not pass this way again.   S. Grellet (1773-1855)

Lives of great men remind us we can make our lives sublime, And departing, leave behind us footprints on the sands of time.   Longfellow, 1807-1882

The bustle in a house
The morning after Death
Is solemnest of industries
Enacted upon Earth.
The sweeping up the Heart
And putting love away
We shall not want to use again
Until Eternity.
Emily Dickinson, 1830-1886

Weeds are flowers blooming in the wrong place.

You may break, you may shatter the vase if you will, but the scent of the roses will hang round it still!

Psalm 17: The breakers of death surged round about me, the destroying floods overwhelmed me; the cords of the nether world enmeshed me, the snares of death overtook me. In my distress, I called upon the Lord and cried out to my God; from his temple he heard by voice, and my cry to him reached his ears.

The earth swayed and quaked; the foundations of the mountains trembled and shook when his wrath flared up. Smoke rose from his nostrils and a devouring fire from his mouth that kindled coals into flame. And he inclined the heavens and came down with dark clouds under his feet. He mounted a cherub and flew, borne on the wings of the wind. And he made darkness the cloak about him; dark, misty rainclouds his wrap. From the brightness of his presence coals were kindled to flame. And the Lord thundered from Heaven; the Most High gave forth his voice; he sent forth his arrows to put them to flight with frequent lightnings he routed them. Then the bed of the sea appeared, and the foundations of the world were laid bare, at the rebuke of the Lord, at the blast of the wind of his wrath. He reached out from on high and grasped me; he drew me out of the deep waters. He rescued me from my might enemy and from my foes, who were too powerful for me. They attacked me in the day of my calamity but the Lord came to my support. He set me free in the open, and rescued me, because he loves me.

SUNRISE, SUNRISES

Where is that little boy/girl I carried?
Where is that boy/girl at play?
I don't remember growing older—
When did they?
When did s/he get to be a beauty
When did s/he grow to be so tall?
Seems like only yesterday
when s/he was small....
Sunrise, sunset, sunrise, sunset
Swiftly fly the days,
Seedlings turn overnight to sunflowers,
Blossoming even as we gaze....
Sunrise, Sunset
Swiftly fly the years,
One season following another,
Laden with happiness and tears.

The lord is my shepherd; I shall not want. In verdant pastures he gives me repose; beside restful waters he leads me; he refreshes my soul. He guides me in right paths for his name's sake. Even though I walk in the dark valley I fear no evil; for you are at my side with your rod and your staff that give me courage. You spread the table before me in the sight of my foes; you anoint my head with oil; my cup overflows. Only goodness and kindness follow me all the days of my life; and I shall dwell in the house of the Lord for years to come.
Psalm 23

CELESTIAL FLIGHT

Can be used for "Astronaut" and "Pilot" Sections of this book

Written about one of the first female American pilots to die while flying during WWII; can also be used for a male pilot

She is not dead—but only flying higher,
Higher than she's flown before,
And earthly limitations
Will hinder her no more.
There is no service ceiling,
Or any fuel range.
And there is no anoxia
Or need for engine change.
Thank God that now her flight can be
To heights her eyes had scanned,
Where she can race with comets,
And buzz the rainbow's band.
For she is universal,
Like courage, love and hope,
And all free, sweet emotions
Of vast and godly scope.
And understand a pilot's fate
Is not the thing she fears,
But rather sadness left behind,
Your heartbreak and your tears.
So all you loved ones, dry your eyes,
Yes, it is wrong that you should grieve,
For she would love your courage more,

And she would want you to believe,
She is not dead.
You should have known
That she is only flying higher,
Higher than she's ever flown.

DESIDERATA

GO PLACIDLY AMID THE NOISE & HASTE, & REMEMBER WHAT PEACE THERE MAY BE IN SILENCE. AS FAR AS POSSIBLE WITHOUT surrender be on good terms with all persons. Speak your truth quietly & clearly; and listen to others, even the dull & ignorant; they too have their story. ෨ Avoid loud & aggressive persons, they are vexations to the spirit. If you compare yourself with others, you may become vain & bitter; for always there will be greater & lesser persons than yourself. Enjoy your achievements as well as your plans. ෨ Keep interested in your own career, however humble; it is a real possession in the changing fortunes of time. Exercise caution in your business affairs; for the world is full of trickery. But let this not blind you to what virtue there is; many persons strive for high ideals; and everywhere life is full of heroism. ෨ Be yourself.. Especially, do not feign affection. Neither be cynical about love; for in the face of all aridity & disenchantment it is perennial as the grass. ෨ Take kindly the counsel of the years, gracefully surrendering the things of youth. Nurture strength of spirit to shield you in sudden misfortune. But do not distress yourself with imaginings. Many fears are born of fatigue & loneliness. Beyond a wholesome discipline, be gentle with yourself. ෨ You are a child of the universe, no less than the trees & the stars; you have a right to be here. And whether or not it is clear to you, no doubt the universe is unfolding as it should. ෨ Therefore be at peace with God, whatever you conceive Him to be, and whatever your labors & aspirations, in the noisy confusion of life keep peace with your soul. ଚ With all its sham, drudgery & broken dreams, it is still a beautiful world. Be careful. Strive to be happy. ଚ ଚ

FOUND IN OLD SAINT PAUL'S CHURCH, BALTIMORE; DATED 1692

Printed in Great Britain
by Amazon